Philosophy of Education:
A Christian Approach

by

Norman De Jong

Presbyterian and Reformed Publishing Co.
Nutley, New Jersey

Dedicated to

Greg
Brian
Amy

Table of Contents

Preface

This book is written for students of education. Others are encouraged to read it, certainly, but those who wish to become teachers or who want to improve their understanding of the educational process, they are the prime readers for whom it is intended. Such an audience, of course, includes those whose love is lost in the labors of professorships.

There are a number of things that this book is not. It is not an encyclopedia of information, purporting to include all that needs to be known in order to become an excellent teacher. There are other, heavier, duller books which will contain those summaries of knowledge for those who might need them. It is not a tightly woven, logically built set of ideas that flows in indestructible progression from beginning to end, comprising a total package which one could then label as a composite educational philosophy. To do that would require a markedly different approach, one which the author has earlier attempted in *Education in the Truth.*

This book is not, either, a prescriptive how-to-do-it catalog of proven methodologies. There are countless numbers of such books on the market, some of them worth the reader's perusal. For those who are ready to enter the classroom or who have already experienced that mixture of joy and frustrations called teaching, there is ample supply of such books already on the shelves.

Philosophy of Education: A Christian Approach is an attempt merely to approach some of the perennial, nagging questions of pedagogy that the serious student of education is certain to encounter. Having taught at the college and university levels for some nine years, and having spent a comparable number of years at the elementary and secondary levels where the most formative teaching occurs, the conviction runs deep that the questions and issues confronted here need to be understood clearly if overwhelming frustration is to be avoided. There are those, to be sure, who never think deeply about common problems and yet survive in the classroom for decades. Those kind are of at least two types: the dull, unthinking ones who transmit their prescribed subject matter from day to day and collect their biweekly payroll while getting their emotional rewards from pursuing the latest fads and myths that have been foisted on the educational scene. For them the grand solution lies just ahead, to be featured certainly in next year's catalogs or prescribed at the next subject-centered convention. The second type are those who are "born teachers," who do almost all the right things in the classroom almost unthinkingly, and yet never find the time to analyze or probe beneath the surface of the daily routine.

At some points the book may appear to drift perilously close to the game of semantics. Chapter V, where relativism is discussed, is one such place where that risk is run, but with serious intention. In Christian and pseudo-Christian circles the cry against relativism is often heard, usually as a defense against the uncritically examined ideas of John Dewey and pragmatic philosophy. Granted that Dewey and many of his contemporaries were gravely in error for their assault against absolutes and traditional Protestant theology and morality. The pragmatists and existentialists of the twentieth century are certainly proclaiming a false philosophy, but their thinking is not wrong because they preached the doctrine of relativity. No, their error lies in the fact that they wished to make everything relative to their own human experience rather than to the God who created them. Theirs is the semantic error, for in all honesty they should be preaching the gospel of subjectivism, a position so weak philosophically that few would dare hide under that umbrella.

On the positive side, word meanings are important and can convey to us the most significant concepts, for, in one sense at least, words are all we have been given for communication purposes. Facial expressions and body language, too, are communicating media, but they travel ineffectively over both time and space. Words, consequently, are important and we all would do well to use them with precision and care. To focus on their meanings, then, is both necessary and revealing, sometimes uncovering essential concepts which have long lain under the rubble of confused thinking. Such is certainly the case with "curriculum."

To understand the key elements which comprise the educational endeavor is to equip and prepare oneself for the challenges and turmoil of a world which seems adrift. To know the real meaning of a God-centered education is to have security when everyone else seems to be re-hashing the debates between the subject-centered and child-centered approaches. To fathom the real purpose of congregating in classrooms each day with 25 or 30 little kids is to be able to bear the frustration of knowing that most of the lessons so meticulously presented will soon be forgotten.

To approach education from a Christian perspective and with a philosophical bent is to better equip oneself for a long and fruitful life of service in God's world. That is our intent, with His help, as we proceed.

I

What Is a School?

Philosophers have often been accused of compounding the simple and confusing the obvious. Many times that criticism is accurate, and those who so becloud the issues are deserving of our condemnation. But sometimes the seemingly simple is not really simple at all. Things are not always what they seem to be on the surface, and appearances only serve to mask reality. When such happens, we need, like Plato, to probe beneath the surface to understand the reality that seems at first so clear.

Thus it is with schools and education. Most persons think they can easily define the words *school* and *education*, but when pressed for clear definitions, their tongues become tied and their pens will not produce. Try it yourself.

We often think of education as being synonymous with school. Then we think of school as that building down the street or in the nearest town where we went for eight or twelve years. For some of us, *school* may be the college or university we attended for additional education. But those are only *examples*, and although examples may help to explain, they do not qualify as *definitions*, for definitions need to be big enough in scope so as to take in all the different examples that might be cited. In addition to the above examples, with which most of us are familiar, there are numerous other examples embracing vastly different types of schools. Consider, for instance, seminaries, medical schools, law schools, military academies, and conservatories of music.

Add to that nursing schools, airline pilots schools, dental schools, tax institutes, diesel mechanics schools, colleges of cosmetology, and CIA training centers. These are but a few of the many types available, but it soon becomes apparent that the appearance, the curriculum, the types of classes, and the kinds of learning experienced are vastly different than the elementary or secondary institutions which we so easily associate with the term school.

We might question whether many of the above institutions are really schools or whether they have illegitimately appended the term so as to legitimize their activities. Is the Hartford Institute for training insurance salesmen really a school? Or should all the educational purists stage a march in protest?

The answer, I think, should be obvious. An insurance school, properly conducted, should be as legitimate as an accounting school, a dental school, or an engineering college. When we accept all these as legitimate examples of schools, though, something expansionary has happened to our original concept. No longer can we think of school merely in terms of neat rows of desks, reading exercises, and tests based on the memorization of books and lecture notes. Our definition of school now has to be big enough to encompass the learning of such diverse skills as sermon construction, tooth extraction, sales technique, gun handling, and curling hair, to name but a few.

Schools have often been defined as places where we go to learn. Suppose, then, that I go to our city library to get a book on how to prune our fruit trees. If I sit there in the reading section and learn enough to get the job done, can I then call the library a school? Or suppose the nursing school sends its neophytes into the hospital wards for the bulk of their learning, does the hospital become a school? Or, as so often happens, a high school offers a driver-training course in its curriculum and places its students behind the wheel to traverse the streets of the city. Does the whole world then become a school?

Learning, we all know, is intimately linked with education,

2

and education is associated in our thoughts with schools. But learning, certainly, is not confined to special buildings or particular years of our lives. We are always learning, no matter whether we be 62 years old or a boy on a camp-out. It has even been rumored that learning takes place in traditional schools, although we have all heard serious doubts expressed on that matter.

Jean Jacques Rousseau, in his famous *Emile*, has convincingly argued that schools are not even necessary for learning. Such basic learning as reading, writing, and speaking will naturally occur at certain levels of maturation, he argues, thus making schools into non-essential institutions. Piaget, in our own day, has argued along similar lines, again with persuasive evidence. Although most of us are too impatient to test these hypotheses, all of us know of individuals who have learned the basic skills without the benefit of having been to school.

Schools are not hospitals, though, and neither are they libraries, even though learning and education occur in all such places and in most every other place as well. Schools are still schools, with some peculiar features distinguishing them from hospitals, grocery stores, horse stables, and highways. To argue otherwise would be absurd, for if every place where learning and education occurred were labelled a school, then everything would be a school. And if everything were a school, then all terms would lose all meaning and necessary distinctions would disappear.

But what makes a school different and peculiar? What marks or characteristics does the school possess which separate it from other institutions? Since God has not deemed it important to delineate these details in His specially revealed Word, we must look for these characteristics by using the wisdom and experiences He has given us.

One of the distinctions which is commonly accepted and useful for purposes of definition is that made between *formal* and *informal* education. Since formal education refers, almost universally, to school, we find here a significant clue. Formal, in this usage, refers to *form* or *structure. Informal* means without form, or not having special design. School, then, means a formed or structured education, while informal learning refers to that which is incidental or lacking formal structure.

Using Rousseau's examples and arguments, we are led to see another distinguishing mark of the school. Rousseau has contended that children will learn all the basic skills without the help of schools, if given enough time. The truth of his observation registered clearly with our family only after we had taken an extensive trip through the eastern United States. By touring such places as Gettysburg, Washington, D. C., New York City, and Boston, our children learned a great deal about the early history of our country. We traveled for three weeks and saw much, but that was only a small part of what there was to learn. We missed far more than what we had time to see, a fact which led to serious reflection. By using such available media as films, slides, textbooks and lectures, we could have learned a great deal more in the same period of time, at considerably less expense and effort. Weighing the advantages and disadvantages of each approach, we were forced to conclude that learning at school is much *faster.* School learning, by the very fact of its being structured, is *accelerated* or speeded up so that more can be learned within a shorter time. Without judging the comparative quality of formal or informal learning, we begin to understand why schools are so important in Western society. We simply do not have the time to wait until a child is 12 or 15 years old before he learns to read. No, if a child is going to function adequately in our excessively complex culture, he must learn to read as early as possible, preferably by the age of 6 or 7. So, too, he cannot afford to learn the skills of driving a car at age 25 or 30 because his work opportunities depend on his being able to drive a car much earlier. At least we think that way.

By organizing and structuring the school's learning activities, we definitely speed up the learning process. Each year at school, as we get caught up in the rush of schedules and activities, we hear people complain about the "rat-race" and express a deep longing for the slower pace of vacation periods. We need to keep these feelings in mind, too, when we read books like Ivan Illich's *Deschooling Society*, for he has caught the non-essential character of the school and expressed a potent wish for a less complex society.

A third characteristic of the school emerges if we again reflect on our trip through the historical sites of the eastern states. The children enjoyed that trip and found much of the learning to be exciting, but they were often bored by the long stretches between the places that were important. The seemingly endless ribbons of concrete and the millions of almost identical trees in the Pennsylvania and New York mountains soon proved boring to them.

If we could quickly hop from selected spot to selected spot and eliminate all those inconsequential hours in between.... Ah, there lies a difference! In school we do just that; we flip the page and move from Bunker Hill to Valley Forge. Another turning of the page takes us to the Washington Monument. We change the reels in our projector and take a guided tour of the Senate chambers or a boat tour of the New York waterfront. How compact! How like a can of Florida orange juice on a cold morning in Iowa.

School, like the orange juice, is *concentrated* or *condensed*. All the non-essentials are eliminated for efficient delivery, but they must be restored before consumption if the diet is to be palatable. Therein lies a duty of the teacher, who must infuse the pages of the history book so as to make it live once again. The teacher who fails or refuses to make history (or literature or foreign language) live again will soon prove to be ineffective and not worthy of the pay given.

Schools, then, are *structured*, *accelerated*, *concentrated*, and *condensed* learning centers, designed to promote as much learning as possible within a specified period of time. These characteristics make schools distinguishably different from that which is not school and serve to justify their continued existence. The form, the rate, the focus, and the elimination of unimportant detail are those marks which distinguish formal schooling from informal education.

To deny these characteristics or to try to change the schools so that these marks disappear would be to take away all justification for schools' existence. This was one of the cardinal errors of the Progressive Education Movement during the 1920's and 1930's. They wanted to remake the school so that it was no different from the communities from which the students came. To the extent that they were successful, to that extent the schools lost their justification and parents were to be commended for failing to support redundant institutions. Schools need to be different, or they do not need to be.

Throughout the history of philosophy is woven the debate as to whether "form follows essence" or "essence follows form." The Christian need not get tangled in that web of semantic gymnastics, but he should conclude that essence is not determined by the form that a particular institution takes. The form, the rate, and the other characteristics cited for schools do not determine the essence or purpose or direction of education. Neither can we determine those important considerations by a careful study of existing examples or models, for then we would have no basis on which to choose the best and ignore the rest. Such can only be found by a careful perusal of the Word of God.

Discussion

1. How would our lives be affected if our schools did not continue to exist? Would the quality of life be improved?

2. Have we in America idolized our schools, ascribing to them powers which they do not possess? If so, who is responsible?

3. Are schools mirrors of society? Or are they agents designed to change society? What evidence can you cite?

4. Are schools any better or worse than the communities in which they exist? What are the implications of either choice?

5. Should students be penalized if their parents request their absence for an educational holiday? Do schools have the right to deny such requests?

II

By Whose Authority?

A VW stopped in front of our house yesterday while I was trying to do some exterior painting. A well-dressed mother got out and walked to a cluster of young girls, the 8 to 12 variety, who were playing keep-a-way with a large ball. One young girl was obviously the lady's daughter, for a lengthy and thoroughly pathetic dialogue followed.

"Please say good-bye to your friends now. We have an appointment in fifteen minutes. Hurry, we will be late."

No reply.

"Please stop. You can play with the girls another day."

No reply again, but the mother persistently pleaded. After ten minutes of curb-standing and one-sided dialogue, the mother finally walked to the neighbor's house and requested permission to leave her daughter for an hour while she went on alone. The neighbor did not seem too thrilled, but lacking a good excuse, what does one do in such situations?

A crisis in authority had camped on our curb. I inwardly cried for the pitiful mother who had been vetoed by a ten year old. Controlling the urge to offer some unsolicited advice, I turned to reflect on how many frustrations that girl must cause her teachers at school. I wondered, too, how the mother ever came to such a pitiful state. Was she taught to treat children that way?

The incident turned my thoughts back a few weeks to an unpleasant incident on the campus of our Christian elementary school. Periodically junior high students from the nearby

7

public school scale our fences and take a short-cut to their homes, often purposely disturbing our classes which are still in session. On this particular day I happened to apprehend a seventh grade boy in mid-transit. His excessively long, unkept hair did nothing to attract me while his rambling discourse of vulgarities and expletives served to repel me. In response to my reminders about locked gates and private property, he proceeded with a defense that was current, popular with his peers, but totally without legal weight. Stripped and cleaned to its essentials, it amounted to the idea that nobody had the right to tell him what he might or might not do. He was his own personal law-maker. According to him, there was not, and could not be, any higher authority which could direct his life. He was sovereign to himself, or so he claimed.

The examples cited above are not unique or unusual in our late-twentieth century culture. Their prevalence, I assume, motivated Dobson to choose *Dare to Discipline* as the title of his excellent best seller. In non-Christian classrooms the preponderance of these types has led teachers to resort to the gimmicks of Skinner's behavior modification and down the slippery road of least resistance. Too many, too, have closed their eyes to the problem with the simple prayer that "this also will pass." But since this societal malady did not erupt overnight, we cannot hope to wake up some morning with most children obeying and respecting authority. No, the curse of human autonomy is of long standing, and has been abetted and honored in theoretical circles, filtering down through cultural and educational processes, glorified in too many public writings, and now solidly entrenched in the very thought patterns of many parents and teachers. These adults may decry the youthful manifestations and the strain it puts on their limits of tolerance, but they are neither ready nor able to critique the question of authority at its conceptual base.

We could legitimately identify the most flagrant proponents of the individual autonomy idea, starting with the American Civil Liberties Union (ACLU). Pushing further up the ladder we could berate the Progressive Education move-

8

movement of the 1930's and 1940's, condemning the gospel of democratic living so ardently advocated by John Dewey, Boyd Bode, William Kilpatrick, et al., but we need not stop there. Beyond them we could point to their sources in the writings of Ben Franklin, Thomas Jefferson, and Tom Paine, all the while tearing apart their almost sacred doctrine of "no government without the consent of the governed."

Such efforts might be beneficial, but while we engage in dissecting America's sacrosanct philosophy of democracy, the problem continues and more youths accelerate their trips to our centers of temporary incarceration.

The Question Is Complex

Lest we think that the crisis of authority is relatively simple and limited to the attitudes of rebellious youths who inhabit our public schools, we need to stop short and look again. Christians are affected too, and not always out of ignorance. Committed children of God, facing real-life concerns in their fields of science, philosophy, education, and parenthood encounter questions that are neither quickly nor easily answered. For example, I was recently reading two opposing magazine articles on the subject of creation, in which both authors claimed to be committed Christians and competent authorities in their field. Both appealed to the Second Law of Thermodynamics and both quoted frequently from the Bible, but they remained unalterably at odds with each other's position.

When reading the magazine, I had a number of options from which to select. I could have read only one of the pieces, accepted the author's claim to authority, and been done with the whole controversial business. His claim to authority, after all, was rooted in a Doctor of Philosophy degree, membership in selected scientific societies, and a faculty position at a prestigious college with a superior academic reputation. The only difficulty was that the other author had an equally convincing claim, counter-balancing his opponent.

A second option would have been to align myself with the

9

Royal Society of Science, so influential in seventeenth century England. They simply rejected, in public pronouncement but not in practice, the notion of all authority. In attempting to avoid the debates that centered around Galileo's and Copernicus' observations, they renounced all authority and put their trust only in empirical observation. Unknown to themselves, they assumed this stance on the advice and under the directed guidance of John Locke. He was, after all, the chief authority on the unreliability of authorities.

In the concerns that trouble our elementary and secondary schools, the options are usually not so abstract and enmeshed with theoretical debate. Because they most often involve known personalities and modes of human behavior, the options reduce to questions of which a person's answer will be most acceptable. Do I accept the offender's defense that he or she is an inviolate person who does not have to bow the knee to any other human being, since all human beings were created equal, with each answerable directly and only to God? Do I accept the teacher's demand that Suzy must obey simply because the teacher has been placed in authority over Suzy? Or do I accede to the parents' demands on the grounds that parental authority always supercedes that of the teacher, who has merely been hired to carry out the parents' prior demands?

Maybe this bothersome debate can be resolved by carefully perusing the state educational code or the latest school law books and thus determining whether a statute has been broken? Knowing of schools which have exercised that option and filled their student handbooks with excerpts from legal documents, we can only conclude that their highest authority has been either the State Assembly or the Supreme Court. Anyone familiar with current legal and juridical practices knows, however, that laws and court decisions are drastically affected by the will of the majority at the time of decision. What has happened, consequentially, is that the authority of law has again been reduced to the will of the most influential persons. Such a reduction does not permit us to ignore the law or to disobey it flagrantly, for God demands clearly that we must obey kings, governors, and all those who are placed in authority over us.

Who Speaks First and Last?

My introduction to the problem of authority should make one thing crystal clear: the question inevitably comes back to a choice of persons. Must I accept the authority of a teacher? a mother? a policeman? a scientist? a judge? a governor? or a philosopher? Must I honor their opinion with respect and obedience, acceding to their demands even though my personal judgment and inclinations might differ sharply? It would be tempting to say a resounding yes, but such an answer would be much too simplistic and probably faulty in specified instances. The caution is necessary because one Person, who has the highest claim to authority, has been ignored. That Person, of course, is God, who is the Alpha and the Omega, the first and the last. As the Person par excellence, He needs to be consulted. Remembering that the word "authority" is built from the root word "author," we need to turn to the Word which God has spoken, for He is the first author of all that has been revealed.

The question of authority, which has been so often enshrouded by the mists of democratic doctrine, is of the type to which the Bible speaks directly. Since the precise use, interpretation and function of the Bible has been a subject for frequent discussion and heated debate, it is first of all necessary that we clarify certain ideas about the Scriptures.

The Bible is only one means by which God reveals Himself. Long before the Bible was written, God's created handiwork revealed His glory, wisdom, power, and goodness (Ps. 19; Rom. 1:20; Matt. 5:44, 45). However, even in the perfect state, this creational revelation was inadequate to give man a clear understanding of God's will for his life. It was necessary for creational revelation to be supplemented with God's direct verbal commands by which man learned that he was to rule the earth, to reproduce, to eat plants for food, to cultivate the garden, and to refrain from eating of the tree of the knowledge of good and evil.

11

After the Fall, the creation was placed under the cloud and darkness of sin. Also, man's ability to discern God's revelation clearly was greatly impaired. Consequently, God's direct verbal revelation assumed an even more central role than it played in the perfect state. God frequently engaged in personal conversation with Noah, Abraham, Isaac, Jacob, and Moses in order to give them guidelines for directing the life and thought of His people.

God no longer talks to individuals in direct personal encounters. He has chosen to lead and guide us today primarily through His written Word. In the Bible, God redeclares His nature as Creator and Sustainer of life in a fuller and clearer way than He reveals Himself in creation itself. But the Bible does not simply republish creational revelation. Rather, it goes far beyond God's original revelation in creation, by revealing God's plan of salvation through the work of Christ, and by revealing God's will for man in this age of reconciliation.

In the Belgic Confession the Bible is referred to as the inerrant *guide for faith and conduct.* By use of a more contemporary analogy, it is helpful to think of it as a *road map* for our journey through life. As such, its scope is life-encompassing, yet its detail is not exhaustive. Like a road map it emphasizes all the important information while ignoring a multitude of details which are not essential to walking or traveling a straight route. Just as it would be foolish to examine a road map for all the county roads, the creeks, the railroad tracks, and the telephone poles, so it would be foolish to expect that the Scriptures will answer questions about plant taxonomy, mathematical sets, seating arrangements for classrooms, or the correctness of a sonnet's form. At the same time, however, it must be remembered that all the crucial insights, the basic principles, and the clear lines of direction are there. In the same vein, it must be remembered that the Bible is a guide to our axiological concerns; it tells us quite explicitly which things are most important and ought to be emphasized. "Seek ye first the Kingdom of God ... and all these other things will be added unto you" is one of the more obvious enjoinders. By emphasizing such required

12

human learnings as love, obedience, sharing our gifts, discerning between truth and falsehood, and by virtually ignoring such manual activities as learning to harness horses, to repair tents, to sow grains, to fish, or to build houses, it gives us a normative set of values which must become ours as we mature.

Within the Protestant heritage it has also been emphasized that Scripture is a *"means* of grace," i.e., an instrument or tool which must be used. God Himself tells us that it is "useful for teaching the truth, rebuking error, correcting faults, and giving instruction for right living" (II Tim. 3:16). It is also the standard by which we can judge the truthfulness or falsity of thought patterns and ideas (Isa. 8:20; Matt. 22:29; Gal. 1:6-9).

What Does Scripture Teach Us?

The above question could be answered in a number of ways, some or all of which would apply specifically to our concerns about authority and the application of it. We could say, for example, that the major motif of the written Word is that of Creation-Fall-Redemption. We might also use the Sin-Salvation-Service theme articulated in the *Heidelberg Catechism.* In order to avoid a needless repetition of commonly accepted theology, however, we ought to look for those answers which will bring about a harmony of position and encourage a positive forward direction.

Unity and Differentiation

One of the significant teachings of Scripture is that the universe which God has made is *one.* This particular emphasis in Scripture is the source of the time-honored Calvinistic insistence on *a* "world and life view," and has served well in refuting the various dualistic positions which have come to challenge orthodox Christianity. Our insistence on the *oneness* of creation is clearly scriptural (see, e.g., Rom. 12; Col. 1; Eph. 4; and I Cor. 12), yet it is also the center of untold confusion. Historically, the confusion stretches back at least to the time of the Pre-Socratic philosophers who had tried to formulate a cosmology based on the concept that all reality is one. One of the leaders in that movement was Parmenides, who insisted that all reality is indivisible, ultimately reducible to one definable entity. Attempting to formulate an answer to the question of the "one and the many," he posited a response which was debated down through the centuries and never satisfactorily resolved by the various thinkers who refused to use the light of Scripture. Paul, however, writing under the direction of the Holy Spirit, has an answer to those basic questions with which the Greeks had long been wrestling. The key to the whole debate lies in the double meaning of oneness. Oneness for the Parmenideans meant that everything is a continuous, homogeneous body and nothing else. What he and all those who followed in his train failed to recognize is that "one" is an equivocal term and may also mean *unity*. If it could only mean homogeneity or identicality, then all differentiation within the universe would be ultimately impossible. When it refers to unity, though, differentiation is not only possible but clearly implied.

Paul writes to the Greek churches and emphasizes to them the *unity* of God's creation, and specifically of Christ's body. By repeated comparison with the human body he illustrates that the church of Christ has many different parts or members, each with its specific task or duty to perform. These duties or functions are assigned by God for the sake of building and strengthening the body of Christ. Obviously the functions are not identical, yet the goal which is set before the various human agents is shared by all, for this is to be a *cooperative* endeavor. In contemporary parlance this same concept might be articulated as "division of labor," where each does his assigned part in order that the total task might be accomplished.

As expressed in a modern paraphrase, I Corinthians 12 tells us:

Now God gives us many kind of special abilities, but it is the same Holy Spirit who is the source of them all. There are different kinds of service to God, but it is the same Lord we are serving.

14

The Holy Spirit displays God's power through each of us as a means of helping the entire church.

Our bodies have many parts, but the many parts make up one body when they are all put together. So it is with the "body" of Christ.

He has made many parts for our bodies and has put each part just where He wants it. What a strange thing a body would be if it had only one part.

If one part suffers, all parts suffer with it, and if one part is honored, all the parts are glad (vs. 4, 5, 7, 12, 18, 19, 26).

Paul's analogy concerning unity and differentiation is in complete harmony with the rest of Scripture, where various passages illustrate the types of functions or duties assigned to specific societal agencies. In Romans 13, I Peter 2, and I Timothy 2, e.g., various duties of the state are defined and the citizens are commanded to respect and obey them, for policemen and governors are established and authorized by God to do His Work. Government officials, whether at the federal, state or local levels, do not derive their power or authority *from the people*, but *from God* who delegates it to them through law-abiding citizens as they carry out their responsibilities.

In Paul's letters to Timothy, among other places, the specific duties and jurisdictions of the instituted church are clearly outlined. To the church officers, specifically, are assigned the particular functions of exercising ecclesiastical discipline and using the "means of grace," i.e., the preaching and teaching of the Word and the administration of the sacraments. Those assignments are not duplicates or carbon copies of each other, but are designed to complement and assist each other.

In numerous places in Scripture God details for His people the assignments He has given to parents. Included in their God-given responsibilities is the task of training and educating the children whom God has given to them. In Deuteronomy 6, Psalm 78, and Hebrews 12, God spells out rather specific guidelines for instruction and discipline.

The importance of a father's responsibility in the education

15

of his children is strongly implied in Paul's letter to Timothy, where he makes the faithful exercise of that duty one of the criteria for selection of officers in the church.

Area Authority

It is only after one has grasped the biblical view of unity and differentiation in life that he can fully understand the scriptural teaching about human authority. Recognition of the unity of life is necessary in order to see that all types of human authority have a single source of origin in God. The ultimate basis of all human authority is to be found in the fact that God created man in His own image and appointed him to be a ruler over the earth (Gen. 1:28). Thus man might serve his Creator. But an understanding of the differentiation of life is also a prerequisite to a proper understanding of authority, for it is on this basis that we see that no man has unlimited authority. Human authority is always exercised under God's ultimate authority and is exercised over only a limited area of life. No man has the authority to play God and become a despot who tries to control completely the life of another person. Nor does any man have authority to give commands contrary to the law of God revealed in Scripture. If he does so, his authority is rendered void by the higher authority of God's law.

Defining the exact limits of a particular area of authority will inevitably be a somewhat controversial matter. One reason for this is because of the considerable overlap of areas (e.g., the overlap between the task of the father as given in Eph. 6:4 and the task of a pastor in Tit. 2 and 3), in the accomplishing of God's will. However, this task is not nearly as controversial as it may seem, for the Scripture speaks very clearly about the responsibilities and limitations of the most basic areas of authority: family, church, and state. It is from God's Word that we learn, for example, that the state has the right to levy taxes upon its citizens, to minister for the public welfare, and to enforce public justice even to the extent of taking away life if necessary (Rom. 13:1-7). However, Scripture is equally clear that if civil authorities ever legislate in a way contrary to the Law of God, the Christian must obey God rather than man (Acts 5:29).

It is necessary to distinguish the primary domains of human authority, i.e., family, church, and state, from more secondary types of authority. The family, church, and state have a character which make them qualitatively different from the forms of authority exercised by a businessman, artist, craftsman, or builder. The following points may help to clarify the distinction:

(1) A person enters into the primary areas of authority by virtue of birth. All children are born into a family relationship and from the moment of birth are regarded as citizens of a country. Likewise, all covenant children are, by virtue of their birth from believing parents, regarded as members of the church of Jesus Christ. Baptism is simply a public confirmation of that state of affairs.

Of course, one may enter a family by means of adoption, or assume citizenship in a new nation, or join the church as an adult convert. But, nevertheless, as a general rule, a person enters these relationships by virtue of birth.

(2) The primary areas of authority are more binding in character than other types of authority. One may easily dismiss a builder or change his place of business, but a child cannot escape the authority of his parents nor the wife the authority of her husband. Although it is possible to renounce one's citizenship and have one's name removed from the rolls of a church, such extreme actions are only rarely done. When they are done, the effects of these primary relationships being severed are much greater in the life of a person than if he cuts up his Ward's credit card and vows to do business with Sears.

(3) It is only in these primary areas of authority—family, church and state—that God has given men the right to punish the disobedient. The father is instructed to use the rod, the church is to exercise discipline, and the state is given the right even to take away life. In contrast to this, a businessman has no right to discipline someone

who laughs at his sales pitch, the artist has no right to punish those who refuse to heed his message, and the builder no right to punish those who reject his work and will not purchase his product.

The above distinctions are very basic in understanding the nature of the authority of the educator. There is no biblical mandate which would oblige us to recognize all educators as functioning *in loco parentis*. However, if one understands the task of the educator *apart from* one of the basic areas of life, then the educator's relationship to the student must be seen as a more secondary type of authority which is analogous to the authority of a businessman. The educator is then one who imparts skills and knowledge for a fee. His authority is limited to maintaining that measure of control in the classroom which is essential for him to carry out his task.

But it is a matter of fact that, with the exception of vocational schools, formal education does not follow this type of pattern. Rather, school membership particularly at the elementary and secondary level, is a relatively binding type of relationship which is not easily broken. Furthermore, the school is generally assumed to have the authority to discipline those who violate the standards of personal conduct of that institution. The teachers and principal, for example, have the right and even the duty to punish students who mar desks, steal from others' possessions, cheat on tests, show disrespect for teachers, or violate dress codes. Although these reasons for disciplinary action have been sharply debated by some and denied by certain court justices, non-public Christian schools still exercise these rights and do so with the authority historically vested in them. The defense of that right is the subject of this entire chapter, but only if we accept the clear Christian teaching that God is the ultimate source of all authority, only then will that defense be acceptable.

At various times in the history of God's people, the instituted church has taken over a significant part of the educational process. During Old Testament times, young boys learned to write (to become scribes) under the tutelage of the

18

synagogue leaders. Later, after the dispersion of the Christians throughout Asia Minor, the church was instrumental in setting up catechetical and catechumenal schools as a religious supplement to the home training. In the early years of America's Calvinistic churches, too, some schools were under the direct supervision of the church, much as they had been during the seventeenth century in Puritan New England. The most common practice, and the one most in harmony with biblical injunctions, nevertheless, is that in which the parents shoulder the primary responsibility which God has given them. In order to carry out this educational mandate in the most efficient and effective manner, parents have cooperatively joined to form school societies and establish schools. Once these societies are formed, the "formal" educational program becomes a cooperative effort and ceases to be an individual matter. The school and the personnel which are employed then operate on behalf of the parents, carrying out their duties *in loco parentis* and administering "parental rules" on behalf of their students' parents.

When such "private" schools are formed, there should never be a spirit of competition with or independence from the home and the church. On the contrary, the school must strive to cooperate with the home and the church in order that their common goals may be reached. Failure to keep sight of this principle causes serious problems in those Christian schools who believe it is their duty to proselytize and do not require that their students come from Christian homes. In such cases the parents and teachers are working at cross purposes, each hoping that their values and perspective will remain dominant. Thus teamwork or cooperation is the first order of business when educating children. Sometimes, of course, that harmonious relationship breaks down, but the occasional violation of a basic principle never negates that principle. Such violation simply illustrates the necessity of that principle and calls us to more consistent application of it.

A school is not a church. Neither is it a home, nor a radio station, nor a cafe, nor a court for petty crimes, nor a training

19

ground for professional athletes, nor a stage for dramatic production. It is not *defined* as any of these, yet whenever the campus scene is analyzed, all the above types of activity come quickly into focus and might be incorporated into the full meaning of "school." Using Paul's oft-repeated analogy again, the Christian educational institution is comparable to the hand, where skin, blood, bones, tendons, and muscles all exist in beautiful union. The various parts are not identical, for then the hand would be skin, and the skin would be blood. By means of analysis we know that the various parts are truly different, but we also know that any attempt to separate and isolate those sundry parts would quickly result in the hand's destruction.

Give Us Freedom!

The school, then, is not a simple institution designed to perform only one or two functions. On the contrary, it is a highly complex institution rightly entrusted and charged with multiple functions. It must teach children to read, to write, and to do arithmetic. But in so doing it must also teach the child to listen, to follow directions, to develop various skills of communication, to pray, to respect authority, and a host of other important things.

But where does the school get the authority to do all these things? Merely by common consent? Do parents consciously and thoughtfully prescribe each of those duties and then invest the teachers with their authority to so do? Do children analyze their needs, consent to be governed in such fashion, and thereby request that someone be placed in authority over them? The answer is obviously in the negative, as anyone who has worked in schools for long knows.

One of the most frequent demands made by persons in western society is the demand for freedom. That demand has frequently been heard on Christian campuses, too, but it seldom blossoms from a sound understanding of biblical directive. Rather, it tends to stem from the cardinal principles of democracy, where the "consent of the governed" and the "sovereignty of man" are incessantly preached.

20

Scripture tells us plainly that God made Adam and Eve good and free. When sin was committed, though, that freedom was lost and man was subject to restraint. When Christ came, He clearly proclaimed that He came "to make man free" (see John 8), to give liberty through the perfect obedience which He offered. The implication is clear: only the Christian who accepts Christ's vicarious atonement and promises to live a life of obedient service can truly enjoy freedom. Since they receive it as a free gift of grace, it is unnecessary, and probably indicative of a wrong relationship to Christ, to demand it.

Since Christ came not to destroy or abolish the law, but rather to fulfill it, freedom comes not apart from law, but always within a framework of it. Our Lord articulates this clearly when He enjoins us with, "If you love Me, keep My commandments." God's frequent demands that children and adults obey and respect those placed in authority over them are never in contradiction with Christ's promise to set men free. No, those two scriptural emphases are in complete harmony, for liberty and law are complementary.

Although God is ultimately the author of all law, He nevertheless gives man responsibility in forming that law according to present needs. Man thus serves as God's temporal agent. In carrying out that law-making function man frequently perverts and distorts the will of God, formulating laws which are in direct contradiction with other laws and making it logically impossible to obey one without violating another. In spite of such predicaments, humans must admit that all are equal under the law and before God. No man may be excused from the demands of the law because of wealth, position, or social standing.

One of the primary demands which resounds through Scripture is that of obedience. Those who have been influenced by democratic thinking find this difficult to accept, but allegiance to that demand has been frequently demonstrated in the practice of both church and civil government. In both of those areas of activity, a person must demonstrate that he is a law-abider before he may become a law-maker.

Furthermore, any instance of law-breaking results in a temporary or permanent denial of voting rights and law-making privileges. Again, the execution of this principle has not been universally or consistently followed, but, by the grace of God, it remains a guiding principle for both our church and our nation. The same must continue to be true in our school program, where students are denied roles in student government for as long as they are under school, civil or ecclesiastical discipline.

Since all of us are subject to total depravity and original sin, a significant facet of our becoming mature and responsible agents for God is that we learn to know, to love and to respect the law. All of us are prone to do evil, to generate mischief, and to test the rules, but this is usually more evident among the younger students than the older. As the older students demonstrate their law-abiding characteristics, they should be assigned progressively greater measures of responsibility, thus preparing them for the full duties which will eventually be theirs.

A person has to learn to obey just as he has to learn to listen, to sing, to read, to swim, to multiply, to play piano, to speak, to dissect cats and to discern between truth and falsehood. The child *should become* a proficient reader, an effective prophet, a loving servant, a good listener, and a discerning citizen who tests all the spirits, the theories and ideas to see whether they be the pure truth of God or whether they be a twisted, perverted distortion of the truth. Of equal or probably greater importance is God's universal demand that His children become obedient servants who want to do His will. The administration and the faculty are, in the school setting, the primary *means by which* such objectives can be reached.

Within the school each of us has our assigned task to be performed. We, in turn, have different tools or instruments with which we are most competent and which we exercise for the sake of developing those mature persons that God desires in His Kingdom. Our assigned tasks are different and our means of accomplishing them come in wide variety, but our goals should be the same. In full consort with the Christian churches and the Christian homes from which our students come, we should press on toward the high calling of God in Christ Jesus.

Discussion

1. Has your state government ever passed educational legislation that is contrary to your beliefs as a Christian? What are some specific examples? What procedures should be followed in resisting such laws?

2. What are some reasons why state governments should not control our schools to the extent that they presently do? Why has this excessive control developed?

3. Since public school teachers are legal agents of the state, what restrictions do they experience which are not shared by non-public school teachers?

4. What are the dangers or advantages of a school controlled by the clergy?

5. How should a Christian define freedom? How is freedom usually understood in our secular society? What are the errors in that secular concept?

6. What are the implications of the idea that law-abiding must precede law-making? What happens if these two attitudes are reversed? Which attitude is prevalent in democratic philosophy?

III

Who Has the Right to Change a Child?

Questions regarding authority tend to arise only under certain circumstances. Seldom, if ever, do they occur in the middle of a teacher's explanation about the process of two-column addition or the geography of Australia. Non-controversial subjects do not produce controversial issues. But supposing the teacher tries to establish the veracity of the creationist position among a class of students schooled in evolutionary theory, then the question of authority will surface repeatedly and not easily be put down.

In a creationist-evolutionist debate, the protagonists are trying to change someone else's mind. Naturally there is resistance, for we all prefer to hold fast to that which has been previously accepted and which now is mentally stored in more or less neat array. To change our minds is to recognize as false that which we now believe to be true. Such repentance comes slowly and painfully, producing the oft-heard question: by whose authority do you make these claims?

Throughout the Gospels the question of authority is raised frequently, most often aimed at Jesus as He pressed His claims to the Godhead on the resisting scribes and Pharisees. When Christ and His disciples taught the message that He was the Messiah, the Jews first had to repent from their prior beliefs before they could believe Him and accept His claims. Their usual response was to demand an explanation directly related to His authority. Those experiences of the Master

Teacher are not unrelated to the daily concerns of the contemporary classroom.

When all the methodological techniques and superficial concerns are stripped away and schooling is reduced to its essentials, one primary characteristic stands out starkly. To teach someone is to change someone. Not normally a drastic revision, but a gradual transformation by the daily renewing of the mind. A change of idea here, a change of thought pattern there, a change of attitude today, and a modification of behavior tomorrow. Slowly, sporadically, patiently, molding and shaping the man of God, completely equipping him for every good work. Putting aside the whims and fancies and ignorance of childhood, all the while replacing them with the wisdom, the understandings, the insights and values of a rich biblical perspective.

That unique Christian vision struck home again one day as I listened to a fourth grade teacher analyze a recent transfer student. He had made the adjustment from an open classroom quite well. No longer did he feel the need to be boisterous and demanding to get the attention he desired. He felt accepted now, but his general deportment and academic progress were still noticeably deficient. As the teacher talked, oblivious to her own choice of terminology, the word "change" was used again and again. By every indication the analysis was precise and correct, but that factor was overshadowed by the central thrust of her description. William still needed to change in so many ways before a report card full of satisfactory grades would indicate warm approval and wholehearted praise.

Does a teacher have that right? May a school set a prescribed standard of behavior and academic excellence, cajoling and coercing the students to conform until they measure up to that standard? Or does such an approach to education violate the sacred right of the sovereign individual? In one form or another, those are cardinal questions which separate the prevailing mentality of the public school from the mind of the Christian educators in late twentieth century society. The difference is huge, coming to practical expressions in such matters as classroom organization, acceptable modes of behavior, curriculum requirements, disciplinary strategies, dress codes, grading practices, and teacher expectancies.

The Christian assumes that right. Without it, teaching would be an exercise in futility. But the Christian need not merely assume, for God has authorized such a stance and has adequately spelled it out in such passages as Proverbs 22, Romans 12, Ephesians 4, and Hebrews 12. Train up a child in the way he wants to go is a devious and devilish perversion, not befitting the mind of parent, teacher or student.

Some years ago a Big Ten university paper published a series of interviews with students who had recently returned from their holiday vacations. The prime questions which the interviewer asked were: first, has the university changed you in any way, and, second, how did your parents react to these changes? The answers to the first question were all highly positive, but varied in the examples cited. New and different attitudes toward traditional morality were mentioned, as were more negative attitudes toward institutional religion. The parental response in many cases was reported as anything but positive. Without attempting to justify the university's blatant disclosure of its sometimes devious work, the reporter simply called attention to what a time-lapse had made obvious. During the short semester in which the students had been away from their homes, they had imbibed many ideas and concepts which their parents and friends found strange if not repugnant.

For better or for worse, a concentrated dose of new ideas and different visions affects the students at whom they are directed. To teach youth is to control the future of a nation, or at least an era in that nation's history. To teach is to bend or twist the tender seedling so as to make the tree inclined. Those who think often or seriously about education, know that. The American Federation of Teachers knows that. So does the National Education Association, the American Civil Liberties Union, the Russian Politburo, the Catholic church, and hosts of others besides. Some parents know it, too, but countless others seem impervious to the competing demands of societal groups, burying their heads meanwhile in the ignorant assumption that schools are simply places where children learn the three R's.

Who Should Control the Schools?

Because the school has historically been the object of power-hungry controllers, it is imperative that Christians keenly understand the issues and take a firm stand on solid biblical ground. In its most basic language, this is the position of parent-controlled schools. In many Christian school circles, the parents of the children enrolled have retained their rights and duties, investing their authority in a Board of Directors, to whom they have delegated power to act. Adhering to that basic stance are such associations as the National Union of Christian Schools, and the Western Association of Christian Schools. Similar consolidated organizations exist in Australia, in Canada, and the Netherlands. These associations have advocated, with numerous biblical evidences, that it is to the parent specifically (but not exclusively) that God has given the mandate to train up a child and to educate him in the way he should walk.

In contrast with this are the positions of such groups as Roman Catholics and Missouri Synod Lutherans. In their frame of reference, it is the clergy that bears the responsibility of organizing and maintaining schools. Although the Catholic clerics, since Vatican II, are gradually giving parents more voice and authority, they have not yet divested themselves of the dominant authority role. Amongst many of the newly emerging Baptist schools one finds a similar ambivalent attitude toward authority, but their positions need not give undue alarm to the Christian community.

What should cause fear and concern is the attitude and ideological position which seeks to wrest responsibility away from both the parents and the clergy, arguing as it does that the school derives its responsibility directly and only from God Himself. Such a position sounds pious enough and can even be supported by selective quoting from Scripture, but the actual implementation bears out its truly insidious

27

nature. The primary proponents of this point of view in recent times have been the members of the Association for the Advancement of Christian Scholarship (AACS) and the adherents to the Cosmonomic philosophy. This idealogical stance first surfaced in the Netherlands during the 1880's and 1890's and has since had a significant rebirth in the post-World War II era. Within the 60's and 70's it has spread from its Canadian base at Toronto to affect seriously the campuses of Trinity, Geneva, Dordt, Calvin and Covenant Colleges, as well as spreading to many elementary and secondary Christian schools in Canada, the United States, and Australia. The National Union of Christian Schools has come under particular attack because this idealogy has surfaced primarily within its own ranks.

This newly emergent attitude toward educational authority is most succinctly defined as "sphere sovereignty." Reduced to its essentials, it argues that each societal agency is an independent, autonomous, sovereign unit answerable to no one other than God Himself. This contrasts sharply with the traditional Christian school position which has long declared the school to be an extension of the home, with primary responsibility for education resting with the parents of the children to be educated.

The Historical Background

In order to comprehend fully the direction and the influence of the AACS and their peculiar position on authority, one needs to understand the major branches within the Reformed and Christian Reformed churches of the Netherlands during the late nineteenth century. From 1852 to 1890, Dutch politics, in which Calvinists were increasingly involved, was preoccupied with religious rivalry, and the question of control of education became the central theme. Continually beset by quarrels between Calvinists and Catholics, the Dutch government had to grapple with problems of ecclesiastical control over education and of religious instruction in the schools. As a growing spirit of democracy gradually overcame the Dutch Calvinists, they became increasingly disenchanted with the power vested in the king and resented his normal control over the schools of the land.

The dominant Reformed thinker in this critical Dutch setting was Abraham Kuyper, who was later to become the Prime Minister of the Netherlands. Strongly attracted to the new democratic philosophy and stridently opposed to the authoritarianism vested in the king, he fully committed himself to a program designed to change the general political situation in the Netherlands.

In response to the many debates going on at the time, Kuyper appealed to the principle of "sphere sovereignty," first enunciated by Johannes Althusius in 1603. Concerned with developing a philosophy of politics, Althusius had stressed the importance of recognizing that on the basis of God's *creational-laws* the various spheres in society have their own internal principles and laws of regulation. In an intuitive leap of faith, Kuyper attempted to apply this concept to all of societal life: the state, the church, the home, the school, industry, science, and art. He developed the concept more fully in 1880 in his famous opening address of the Free University, basing his comments on I Corinthians 15:23: "But every man in his own order. . . ."

Although this passage speaks primarily about the death and resurrection of Christians, Kuyper twisted it to explain why the church, the state, the school and other areas of life should be considered independent and free from any domination or control by any other societal institution. Clearly it was not an exegetical exercise, but a political response to a political situation by an active politician. By attempting to merge the principle of divine sovereignty with the political philosophy and natural-law idea of Althusius, Kuyper hoped to wrest educational control away from both the Dutch government and the ecclesiastical groups that had quarreled over it for two decades. To claim that the school possessed its own sovereignty was to deny the claims of all competing parties.

In the Netherlands Kuyper had his strong supporters and disciples. Among them were Dr. Herman Dooyeweerd and

Dr. D. H. Vollenhoven. During the first half of the twentieth century they attempted to extend and develop Kuyper's concept of sphere sovereignty, applying it not only to human societal life, but to all of created reality. The resulting philosophy has variously been labeled as the Cosmonomic Idea, the Philosophy of Law, or the Dooyeweerdian philosophy. Its primary advocates are the members of the Association for the Advancement of Christian Scholarship, headquartered in Toronto. Its leading spokesmen are Dutch immigrants who came to America after World War II and who received their discipleship at the Free University of Amsterdam. It is this group in particular which has condemned the traditional Christian understanding of educational authority and responsibility, causing untold difficulties amongst Christian school supporters.

Kuyper's philosophy also generated a great deal of opposition, both in the Netherlands and in North America. Much of this opposition again surfaced between 1969 and 1975, when AACS advocates tried to change the Constitution of the National Union of Christian Schools and attempted to force their thinking on the Christian college communities where they had gained academic entrance.

Although the AACS people make claims to the contrary, the sphere sovereignty position has not been granted a place in Reformed, Calvinistic theology. It is not expounded or even mentioned in John Calvin's writing, the Heidelberg Catechism, Canons of Dort, the Belgic Confession, or the Westminster Confession. Such outstanding Calvinistic theologians as Warfield, Hodge, Berkhof, Hoeksema, and Heyns do not even bother to mention it. Since the beginning of the twentieth century, however, sphere sovereignty has been a part of the Christian Reformed denominational heritage. For the most part, though, it has laid dormant and has only surfaced in certain stress situations (e.g., the parochial statues of Calvin College and the AACS debate at Dordt College) and in the writings of certain ardent spokesmen for the Kuyperian position. For the most part, sphere sovereignty is still almost exclusively a *scholastic* doctrine, i.e., one debated by schoolmen and largely ignored by or even unknown to those outside of college settings.

What Errors Does It Espouse?

The concept of sphere sovereignty or institutional autonomy raises serious questions and demonstrates significant confusion which cannot be ignored. The first major area of confusion involves an understanding of the principle of unity and differentiation. My understanding of that principle is enunciated in the pages of Chapter II. In this enunciation the first emphasis is on unity or the oneness or wholeness of God's creation. One begins with the wholeness and then, and only then, proceeds to look at the differentiated parts which comprise that unity.

The sphere sovereignty spokesmen begin by emphasizing the differentiated parts and label them each as being *sovereign*, *independent*, *limited*, and *coordinate*. Only after that does there come an emphasis on the unity which must presumably be asserted. Now, however, having asserted independence and sovereignty, unity must somehow or other be established. Separateness is presupposed, so now a "struggle" must be carried on to build bridges, to assert unity, and to bind together in philosophical matrimony that which God never joined in the first place.

If we are to take institutional autonomy seriously and apply the adjectives which are provided, the following picture emerges:

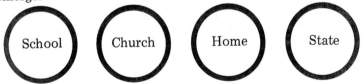

Fig. 1 *The Sovereign Social Spheres.* According to Abraham Kuyper and his disciples, each sphere has "the right, the duty, and the power to break and to avenge any resistance it encounters." Furthermore, each social sphere has its own nature, its own laws according to which it must operate, and its own function to perform.

To the above must be added such other sovereign spheres as Science, Art, Business Industry, Commerce and Agriculture. By doing so we have a proliferation of independence and sovereignty and have a "world and life view" that is characterized by disjointed parts.

Fostering and perpetuating such an image of God's world is a dangerous business. The visual image which becomes embedded in people's minds is precisely that picture which secularists have been trying to draw for centuries and against which we so loudly cry.

The sin of secularism has frequently been illustrated in *dualistic* terms, with everything being assigned either to the sacred or the secular. The form that secularism usually takes, however, especially on non-Christian campuses, is much more complex than the dualism described above. Not only is the sacred (God and the Bible) confined to a compartment by itself, but the secular is divided up into numerous independent, sovereign domains, each by itself, often in a fashion almost identical to that described in Figure 1 above.

The resulting situation leaves the various academic departments operating autonomously and the various disciplines unable even to communicate among themselves because of the false assumption that education has nothing to do with history, history has nothing to do with psychology, and psychology has nothing to do with philosophy. The secular presupposition, in short, destroys the university and creates a multiversity. Secular attempts to find unity will never prove satisfying or successful until they accept the coherence of the whole creation in Christ.

Although advocates of sphere sovereignty also recognize the importance of viewing the creation as a unity, it should be apparent that their concept is more a hindrance than a help in attaining that goal.

Is Sovereignty Divisible?

If we are to take the sphere sovereignty concept seriously and assume that the phrase means what it says, we must address ourselves to another question: Is sovereignty divisible?

The question surfaces most poignantly in the writings of Boyd H. Bode, a prominent educational philosopher during the first half of the twentieth century, who departed from the Christian faith and became a disciple of John Dewey. Bode, when confronted with the Kuyperian position, concluded that the answer was to be affirmative. He promptly concluded that both God and man could be sovereign, each in his separate realm. At that point began his conversion to the gospel of democracy, for the sovereignty of man is essential to democratic philosophy. It was not long, though, before Bode re-asked the question, this second time with the conclusion that sovereignty was not divisible, and that some adjustments had to be made. Hanging tenaciously yet to the monism of Calvinism, he decided that man would keep his sovereignty and that God had to be denied.

The meaning of the word sovereignty is quite precise. Standard dictionaries will define the term as follows: (1) chief or highest, supreme; (2) supreme in power, superior in position to all others; (3) independent of, and unlimited by any other. The term has been used, carefully and correctly by John Calvin when he ascribes sovereignty only to God. Various "absolute" monarchs have also tried, albeit erroneously, to append the term to themselves. In our day the term has been appropriated by humanistic masses who preach a doctrine of "popular sovereignty." Each of those usages raises important questions, but their examination will have to wait for another time.

If the sovereignty of each societal sphere is asserted, then the only logical possibility is to make each sphere limited and independent. By definition, one cannot have two highest or supreme authorities within the same domain. Only if one posits separate, limited, independent realms of authority can one talk about a multiplicity of sovereigns, and then only one per sphere. If the spheres should intersect, however, the question must then be raised as to whom is to be sovereign in the area of intersection.

The sphere sovereignty position betrays added confusion on this score, for the advocates of that position insist that the various spheres are not only sovereign and independent, but also somehow interrelated and overlapping. To divide and subdivide the sovereignty which only belongs to God so as to spread it liberally amongst the various societal agencies is to invite men and institutions to operate from the principle of autonomy. What happens, consequently, is that whoever tries to apply the basic concept becomes highly suspicious of and callous toward other authority which seeks to regulate their life. Much of that has already come to expression on our Christian campuses, where some students insist that they have separate, distinct authority merely by virtue of their being an identifiably different part of the school. That mentality did not just happen. It was nurtured and fed by the propagation of an erroneous theory, which the brighter students saw fit to extend logically to their own situation. The results are not pleasant.

Ends—Means

A third major confusion which arises out of the sphere sovereignty concept is that involving *ends* and *means*. Again, this question is centuries old, but in the Neo-Calvinistic tradition this confusion reaches a new intensity, often culminating in the expression, "We must struggle with the issues!" By insisting that we must go to education for educational norms, to literature for literary norms, and to politics for political norms, and, simultaneously, condemning those who look to Scripture for their guidance and direction, the emphasis is again placed on the primacy of the differentiated parts.

Such an insistence causes serious problems at the very practical level, for education is going on almost everywhere, in the home, in the catechism class, by the creek bank, in the legislative halls, in front of television sets, in schools of cosmetology, and on summer vacations. Where does one look, then, for educational direction? By the creek bank?

The contemporary secular insistence that the schools, like all the other autonomous institutions, have their own pre-ordained law, its own prescribed character and function, and its own normative regulations, causes similar serious problems. This insistence bears a striking resemblance to the Platonic "theory of forms" and could be amply supported by quotations from Plato's *Dialogues*, but no such explanation is found in the Bible. In the Scriptures one finds an insistence on common goals or objectives (*ends*) and a definite differentiation of specific duties, but no hint of distinct laws governing and directing each sphere separately.

Protestant theology has long emphasized, too, specific *means*, and that on the basis of biblical evidence. The instituted church, for example, has been assigned by God a very specific *means of grace*, which involves the preaching of the Word, the administration of the sacraments, and the exercise of church discipline. The state, too, has been given particular tasks and is even given "the sword" with which to punish evil.

But what of the *school*, which is only mentioned incidentally in the Bible? Does it have specific duties? Does it have God-prescribed means with which to do its work? Or was God possibly guilty of a major oversight?

I think not. God has given us ample guidance in the Scriptures, so that if we search them diligently, we can find those major guidelines and principles to guide us through the mess that is twentieth century American schooling and help us to operate our schools in a God-glorifying manner.

The most common form of confusion over *ends* and *means* in formal education is expressed in the oft-heard phrase: "I teach history" or "I teach mathematics." Such statements reflect or betray the idea that "history" and "math" are the *ends* of the educational process. If one transfers that type of thinking to the building industry, one would have to say that "Carpenters build hammers" and "Plumbers fix pipe wrenches." Such talk would convince you that the person was confusing his tools (*means*) with his ends or objectives.

The proponents of sphere sovereignty demonstrate a similar confusion, but, unlike the above example, they try to place the means in a position where they can be the *source* of direction, the *source of laws* and of guiding principles. Their theoretical position would be analogous to that of a carpenter who asked his hammer and saw what kind of house he should build or of a farmer who questioned his machinery as to the type of crops he should plant.

What needs to be recognized is that God in His Word has already given us the blueprint. He has told us what kind of persons we *ought to become.* He has stipulated goals and directions for our lives. He has told us that He wants all His children to become loving, discerning, wise, obedient, knowledgable, faithful servants of His. The goals (ends) are then set, pre-determined for us by the Architect of our lives. We can choose to ignore His plan, or we can strive to follow it, but let us never confuse the issue by claiming that the goals or ends for education are still to be discovered somewhere in sovereign education!

If the ends are set, what then of the means? The *primary* means by which God brings us to His appointed end is that of *faith.* By faith God justifies us, frees us, makes us obedient, and helps us become wise, mature servants. The Belgic Confession expresses this so beautifully in Article XXII where it says:

> We do not mean that faith itself justifies us, for it is *only an instrument* with which we embrace Christ our righteousness. And faith is an instrument that keeps us in communion with Him in all His benefits.

But God gives us more than the means of faith. He places us in homes, churches, and schools and uses these so that His creatures may grow up into full Christian maturity, equipped for every good work. The following chart will illustrate the progression of man through life and the way that *ends* and *means* fit the picture.

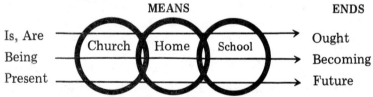

Fig. 2. *The Societal Institutions.* Note here that the three parallel lines are merely alternative or synonymous ways of conveying the same concept. They should not be interpreted to mean three separate lines of development or essentially different ideas.

A major difference between the approach suggested above and that of the sphere sovereignty position is that the emphasis is centered on people and personal development rather than on creational structure. Both the Creation-Fall-Redemption motif of the Neo-Calvinists and the Sin-Salvation-Service theme of the Heidelberg Catechism ought to suggest to the reader that the Bible is much more concerned with people than with creational structure. To the extent that we concentrate our interest on creational structure at the expense of human progression through life, to that extent we throw the Scriptures out of focus.

God is concerned with people primarily, for they are the crown of His creation. With them He has fellowship and for them He sent His Son. To allow or encourage ourselves to be excessively preoccupied with creational form and structure is to minimize that central biblical emphasis on persons. Figure 2 above redirects that emphasis so that the prime attention is paid to the question of human progression through life. The terms on the left side of Figure 2 are illustrative ways of asking the question: "What *is* man?" In practical, concrete ways we must also ask: "What *are* the significant, common, and unique characteristics of those persons with whom we have to do? "What are they like right now *in the present*?"

Our concern, of course, does not stop at that point. To do so would be to endorse, bless and enshrine the status quo. Scriptural injunctions simply will not permit such. We must also ask: "What *ought* these persons *become*?" "What does God demand of us?" "To what has He called us?" Our concerns, then, are always forward-looking. With biblical awareness of God's demands, we become preoccupied with the affects of our actions on students' lives, with the kinds of teachers, parents, ministers, they will become. How can we influence and direct their lives so that they will *become* the stable, mature, joyful, witnessing Christians of which the Bible speaks?

Our specific work assignment and the range of our jurisdiction, of course, is limited. Our function as teachers is not to administer the ecclesiastical sacraments; neither is it to conscript an army, nor to raise taxes.

Our task is to *educate people*. By the grace of God, and often in spite of ourselves, we have been doing that. God has used us, even though we have not often understood what it is we are doing or should be. Our formulation of rules and regulations governing both the academic and non-academic areas of life have been an integral part of that total educational effort. The administering of punishment, too, has been done out of Christian love and concern and with the prayer that through such discipline the students might learn how to live the Christian life.

Discussion

1. What kind of corporate structure should a parent-controlled school adopt so that the parents retain their basic authority over the educational process?

2. Are parents inclined to want the best possible education for their children? Why?

3. How should the demands of an individual parent be handled when such demands conflict with the general policy of the school?

4. Our secular colleges and universities today often assume an autonomous attitude, asserting that they know what is best because they have the necessary expertise. Is authority based on insight, as they claim? If not, what is the source of authority?

5. During the Middle Ages, the newly emergent universities of Europe ascribed to themselves sovereignty and internal regulation. What kinds of problems did this create? What similar problems do our schools today experience?

IV

True or False?

This book constitutes an infinitesimal addition to the mountains of literature available to twentieth century man. It will probably go unnoticed by most, but hopefully it will become armament in the idealogical warfare going on at many schools. I say "idealogical warfare" without hesitation, for such is the essential character of dynamic education, with the library being nothing less than a prime arsenal. Idealogical warfare is, ideally, not to be carried on between the members of a faculty, nor even between faculty and students. Rather, it is a contest for the allegiance of minds to the truth in opposition to the allurements of false philosophies, ideals and prophets.

Idealogical dispute is one of the main explanations for the continuing proliferation of literary material. Without dispute, disagreement, and the conviction that someone else's explanation is false, or at least inadequate, little, if anything, would be written and justification for publishers' existence would rapidly diminish.

Whenever there is a conflict of ideas or concepts, one thing is certain: not all of the ideas or concepts can be right and worthy of acceptance as truth. To illustrate, suppose that I were to argue that the recent Watergate scandal was actually a just and holy action, wrongly exposed by an immoral and hungry press, with Nixon deserving much more sympathy from the American people. Immediately one could expect rebuttal from many sides. The counter-arguments would be numerous, probably rekindling the animosities that wracked our country for years. Or suppose that we were to raise the specter of evolution once again. Some presumed scholars and teachers persist in perpetuating the notion that all life and reality originated with simple, single-celled organisms and managed, somehow, to evolve over millions of years into the wonderfully complex world we see all around us. Thankfully, there is still a large number who stand up to refute such unscientific and illogical nonsense.

It is not our purpose here to investigate these arguments in all their detail. The point is, however, that not all sides can be right; some must be wrong, and there is even a possibility that all may be wrong. Some of the proponents must, of logical necessity, be speaking falsely. It is also possible, and even probable, that some are speaking truly. But who is to decide and how?

One of the poems that has long fascinated me, but which regrettably has been falsely labelled as children's literature, is "The Blind Men and the Elephant" by John G. Saxe. Concerning the symbolic Elephant, these "six men of Indostan, to learning much inclined, . . . Disputed loud and long, Each in his own opinion Exceeding stiff and strong." Is it possible that they were all giving a true description? Saxe wisely concludes, ". . . all were in the wrong!" Each blind man thought he was describing the Elephant truly, but none of them were. The fourth contended, "the Elephant is very like a tree," but he was very certainly mistaken. Could he, though, rightly have argued, "the Elephant's legs are like trees"? Again, no! At best he might have contended that one type of appendage of that organic unity called Elephant is like one part of the wholeness called tree. These six men, in spite of their much learning, or maybe because of it, were emphatically and definitely perpetrating falsehoods.

What was their weakness, their deficiency? They were blind! They could not comprehend the whole Elephant, and what they could grasp, they subtly perverted. At best they could understand one part, one facet, and that they absolutized. They absolutized one aspect and claimed that it explained the whole. They thought they knew the essence of elephantness when they only had a fumbling grasp of the tail.

Such is the situation in our world today, and especially in the world of education. Books, magazines and ideas abound in tidal quantities. "Education is vocational preparation." "No! Education is the honing of the basic skills, the three R's." "On my word! Education is transmission of a cultural heritage from the older to the younger." "You are all wrong!" Education is the experience of becoming democratic citizens. "Pardon my entrance, gentlemen, but education is whatever you, individually or collectively, determine it to be."

Such is the rising crescendo of argument in pedagogical circles. "Whom and what do I believe?" is the dilemma of the questing student. "Can I believe everyone I read and hear? They cannot all be true. Are they all false? Is each one totally wrong?"

Blindness to the truth is not novel to twentieth century man, and certainly not unique to America. School curriculums are, at least in part, a record of intellectual disagreement, of ideological confrontation. When such is the content of the school, and unavoidably it is, what is left for the student except either to be horribly confused and pulled mentally asunder, or to fight the good fight of faith?

I have often been intrigued by the reactions of my students to the ideas I present. What do they do with those statements? Do they accept them as true, or do they believe them to be false? Or don't they know what to believe? Does this new idea, just encountered, conflict with previous beliefs? What beliefs do they presently hold? By whom and through what media have they been influenced? What do their facial contortions and their body posture tell me by way of response?

Students never come to school (or to church, for that matter) empty-headed and blank-sheeted. They come burgeoning with ideas and attitudes on sundry and unexpected topics. They derive these from every imaginable source—TV, radio, newspapers, parents, friends, siblings and family trips. Many times they are confused by this bombastic collection and little appreciate our contributions to their mental chaos.

41

At other times they have their thoughts neatly sifted and wish for continued quiet. Then, confronted with our intrusion, their response is one of passive, yet effective resistance.

The possibilities for conceptual dispute are innumerable. This teacher does not agree with that teacher. That teacher does not agree with the textbook author. The textbook author does not agree with yesterday's newspaper article. The newspaper doesn't harmonize with the TV commentator. My father turned him off. And nobody agrees with me. There is so much static! Tune me out! But give me love and peace.

That response should be no cause for surprise and shock. Not knowing what to believe is deeply disturbing and indecision is an excruciating, albeit temporary, psychological condition. Yet "tuning out" is not a desirable response and not long tolerated. Beliefs and ideas, including those presently held by the students, must be examined. We must stop practicing with meaningless facts and get on with the real battle. But is it conscionable for teachers to insist that false ideas be exposed for what they are and that true ideas be identified and accepted as such, even if it requires sundry and persuasive proof by way of argument? Is the teachers' and students' task truly that of pursuing, pinning down, and laying hold of the truth, all the while rejecting the lie?

The Christian community has long been asserting that "neutrality is a myth, an impossibility." Now I am in wholehearted agreement with that assertion, and I believe that we all ought to be, *but*, when are we going to get on with the obverse (the positive counterpart) of that statement? What is the obverse? Simply stated, it is this: *Every idea, concept or belief is either true or false.*

When I present that idea to my students, the variety of their reactions is frequently cause for amusement, yet their initial responses are almost universally negative. The professor flipped, seems to say the look in their eyes. But, if not apriori committed to rejection of such a postulate by the influence of other belief propagators, their questions soon lead to: "Can that be proven?"

The answer is *Yes.* One can certainly find evidence for

such an assertion in Scripture. Scripture brooks no neutrality: "He that is not with Me is against Me." "I am the truth." Such statements, coupled with references to an extrapolations from the biblical theme of the antithesis, do not convince all students, however. Convinced that there is flaw in our interpretation or leap in our logic, they remain hesitant and skeptical. Although not daring to articulate it, the lack of acceptance is tacit expression of their belief that you have spoken falsely.

There is added evidence for such skeptics in simple logical terms. It can be succinctly stated in the following way:

1. If an idea or concept is true, then it is true.
2. If an idea or concept is not true, then it is not true.
3. Not true means false.
4. If an idea were neutral, then it would be not true. (If it were true, then it would be true and not neutral.)
5. If that idea were not true, then it would be false.

One could continue with such gymnastics, but the point should be clear. Neutrality, in the sense of a proposition being neither true nor false, is an impossibility, just as orthodox Christians have long asserted.

When we come to recognize the truth of the statement that every idea is either true or false, we must also recognize the necessity of certain fundamental principles which will temper our judgments. Some of these principles are:

First, truth or falsehood is not dependent on our believing it to be true or false. Even if every white person firmly believed the Negro to be innately inferior, as some whites are still inclined to feel, all that belief would not change the truth of the matter. Truth and falsehood are not determined by majority vote.

Second, we cannot intelligently, accurately, wisely decide if an idea is true or false until we understand what is meant by the words, phrases and symbols that express that idea. Many times we should ask for clarification, for clearer understanding, before we come to a personal decision. For example, the statement, "The Bible is not a textbook for science" has caused no little conflict in some circles. Is that true? Or is

43

it false? Before accord and peace can be reached, the meaning of at least two words (textbook and science) should be articulated. Pressing such demands, however, may lead to diversionary but not unfruitful conflict, while the original issue remains in limbo.

Third, to assert that every idea or concept is either true or false is not to assert that we know which to be true and which to be false. Many times we will simply have to admit that we do not know. In fact, we may have real difficulty in coming to a decision. When confronted with conflicting ideas where the choice is not easy, we are disturbed and slowed down. But decide we must, for prolonged skepticism is antithetical to man as believer. Our students often experience this even though we may be oblivious to their trauma. They may still be trying to decide a particular matter while we have traveled on, unconscious of their blank stare or furrowed brow.

Fourth, much truth and falsehood are shared by regenerate (Christian) and unregenerate (non-Christian) alike. This is simply another way of saying that there are many truths on which men of differing faiths find agreement or common acceptance. That the Pilgrims landed at Plymouth Rock in 1620 is not apt to cause a war of words, but neither does the common acceptance of that belief warrant the labelling of that idea as "neutral." Neither common acceptance of truth as truth nor even common acceptance of falsehood as truth can be construed to equal neutrality.

If, however, neutrality were limited to meaning the absence of conflict, then we would have to agree that some simple propositions, devoid of real significance, are neutral. But that meaning of neutrality is not the one against which the Christian must militate. What the child of God must be on guard against is the perverted notion that truth and falsehood are not important and that a person should be allowed to believe whatever seems true or convenient to him. Such a notion is a subtle and very prevalent tool of the devil.

Fifth, truth and falsehood, as discussed here or elsewhere, can not merely mean an accurate or inaccurate account of

44

the actual or objective state of affairs. It is certainly that, but truth and falsehood must mean much more. If we did not assert this latter belief, we could rightly be charged with fragmenting and dissecting what is intended and created whole. If we do not recognize truth as more than accurate description, our ideological wars will not bring peace and victory; they will leave us collecting shrapnel for condolence. Falsehood, too, has expanded meaning and can best be understood as all the prevaricating work of the devil.

The nature of falsehood and evil has often been debated through the ages. St. Augustine wrestled long with the idea and briefly accepted the explanation offered by a Babylonian priest, since called Manichaeism. This Christian heresy tried to explain falsehood by emphasizing the eternal conflict between Light and Darkness, Good and Evil, God and Satan. The idea sounded plausible enough to Augustine, but he soon found it necessary to explain the origin of evil and falsehood, for Mani had asserted that truth and falsehood were two separate, independent entities. Goodness and truth and light were creations of God, of that Augustine was certain. But where did falsehood and evil originate? Did not God create everything? Was it not Christ who made *everything* in heaven and on earth?

This "problem" has not disappeared for many Christians even today. And philosophers have not been without their supposed answers. Some have asserted that falsehood is merely the absence of truth, and evil the absence of good. This position, too, raises difficult questions about the cause or origin of such an absence, questions that are impossible to harmonize with the givens of Scripture.

The only answer that seems to be satisfactory is to view falsehood as the perversion or prevarication of truth. Since *all* things originated with God at the time of Creation, and since God cannot be charged with creating falsehood or evil, we must come to recognize that what was originally good and perfect has since been twisted, distorted, or perverted so that it no longer honors God and reflects His perfection. This Satan did already in the Garden of Eden, taking a perfectly good law of God and subtly twisting it so that Adam and Eve were trapped by it.

Satan is still the father of lies and the great perverter of truth. Twisting the truth ever so slightly, he makes the lie seem so wholly agreeable. In a state of sin, man prefers the lie and suppresses the truth in unrighteousness. To the Christian, however, the lie must be exposed as falsehood, which can only be done when it is tested against the perfect revelation of God. That perfect revelation of God is truth, still manifested without distortion or perversion in the Word of God and in the Incarnate Christ. For that reason, Christ could assert, "I am the truth, the way, and the life." For that reason, too, God could claim, "My Word is truth."

God has told us that He is never absent from us and that His Spirit will guide us into all truth. This is a tremendous comfort for the Christian student as he seeks to know the truth which will make him free. But Satan is never far behind. He is real and active wherever students learn. He uses teachers, textbook authors, government pamphlets, and newspaper reporters. The devil twists the truth ever so slightly and often tries to hide it, but seldom does he use the obvious, for then falsehood would be clearly falsehood and few would be led astray. A 2 degree turning away from the truth is more to his liking, for a 90 degree turn would wake up the wary. For this reason, students don't suddenly forsake the faith. No, they drift away by degrees, all the while comforted by the knowledge that they are still so close to the truth.

Understanding truth and falsehood is crucial in Christian education, but there is still another fundamental principle that needs attention. Without it, the fight of faith cannot result in complete victory. Although it has been rejected by numerous Christians and long held captive by the enemies of God, its reclamation is imperative. Its most simple formulation is this: *All truth is relative.* Since this concept is so important and can easily be misunderstood, a separate chapter will be devoted to it.

Discussion

1. Assuming the truth of the statement, "all ideas are either true or false," what are the implications for teaching?

2. Why does God warn us in Scripture that not many of us should be teachers? What kind of punishment is promised for those who lead little ones astray?

3. How can teachers most effectively discover or determine the present beliefs of their students?

4. Is it essential to learning that there be a change of mind on the part of the learner? Consult Romans 12:1-2 and Ephesians 4:22-24.

5. What types of resistance may a student display if he encounters an idea or practice which is posited as true, but which he believes to be false?

6. What is meant by critical reading? Is its purpose that of ascertaining the truth or falsity of the printed idea? Do our schools sufficiently focus on such skills?

7. What is wisdom? How does it relate to truth?

V

Relativism: A Christian Position

Please do the following exercise before you do anything else. Simply circle the T or F before each statement, indicating whether each is true or false.

T F 1. The curved line at the end of this sentence is a convex line.)

T F 2. The curved line at the end of this sentence is a concave line.)

T F 3. Green Lake in Wisconsin is a large body of water.

T F 4. Lake Michigan is a large body of water.

T F 5. The Pacific Ocean is a large body of water.

T F 6. Freezing temperature is reached when the thermometer registers 32 degrees.

T F 7. That car, traveling 40 MPH, is going very fast.

T F 8. At the time this quiz was composed, it was Wednesday, July 9, 1975, 2:00 P.M. (Please assume the author's honesty.)

T F 9. Gerald R. Ford, the President of the U.S., is a nephew.

T F 10. If you travel due north and continue in a straight line, you will travel north indefinitely.

T F 11. It is now either the spring or the summer season.

T F 12. My present weight is _____ pounds. (Please fill in your own accurate weight, as it registers on earth.)

48

How many of the above statements did you mark as true? How many false? With how many did you have difficulty?

Simple quizzes, constructed in the same format as that used above, are common in our schools. Frequently, though, the bright students who normally did "A" work would want to ask questions during the quiz and often embarrassed the teachers in front of the other students. If denied the privilege, they would get a high percentage wrong and then feel very frustrated with the teacher. Watch those kids carefully, for without proper understanding, those normally bright students will soon become prime disciples of pragmatism and drift away from the Christian faith.

I have known too many well-meaning teachers who, when confronted with the above situation, would simply assume self-righteous indignation and condemn those smart-alec kids who had yet to learn to respect authority. But such teachers are not yet wise, for the questions above, and countless others like them, are not easily answered. If I had to take the above quiz and have the grade entered in a school's record book, I would probably refuse to take it and ask instead for a conference with the teacher. Why? Because every one of those statements is *relative* and could be answered as either true or false, depending on the student's perspective.

Is that heresy? Is that in conflict with the preceding chapter? I think not, even though it sounds deceptively similar to the arguments long since advanced by William James and John Dewey, the popular American pragmatists. They loved to pose such questions, watch their students squirm, and then offer a pallet of answers which the Christian should never accept. They, like so many persons operating in our secular schools today, grew up in Christian homes but then renounced God and spent the rest of their days leading the curious down a primrose path to doubt and destruction. Their questions, nevertheless, were legitimate, but their answers were misleading.

Turn back to the quiz again. If you did not notice the first time, please consider the following observations:

1 & 2	The terms "convex" and "Concave" are *relative* terms, depending on where you stand *in relationship to* the curve. When moving from one side of the line to the other, the descriptive term must be changed because, by definition, convex means that which is curved outward, away from the point of reference.
3, 4 & 5	Green Lake is very small in comparison to either Lake Michigan or the Pacific. Green Lake is, by contrast, very large when compared to some of the other lakes in its immediate vicinity. It could also be argued that Green Lake is a town and therefore not a lake at all.
6	The thermometer may register 32 degrees, but that is nowhere near freezing if you are using either a Centigrade or a Reaumur thermometer. Even on the Fahrenheit scale the 32 degrees applies only to water and not to such other liquids as gasoline or alcohol.
7	40 MPH would be very fast in a busy school crossing, but would be too slow for most of our freeway travel.
8	It was 2:00 P.M. in Los Angeles, but it was 4:00 P.M. in Chicago and 5:00 P.M. in New York. What day was it in Tokyo? In London, England?

The remaining questions pose similar problems which the reader can discover for himself, but the point should be obvious. There are questions of relativity which simply can not be ignored, and the brighter students to whom God has given keen insight should be encouraged to exercise their legitimate curiosity.

But what then of Dewey, James, and their pragmatic position? Is all truth relative? Are there no absolutes? Is truth fluid and never fixed, subject only to the whim of the person currently making the judgment? Is beauty in the eye of the beholder and truth whatever seems true to a given person at a given time?

In partial consort with the pragmatists, *the Christian must recognize that all truth is relative*, but from that point on he must take issue with obviously non-Christian thought. It clearly does not follow, logically or epistemologically, that because truth is relative there are no longer any absolutes. What pragmatists have done is to subtly pervert the truth, twisting it slightly after an innocent opening assertion. A classic example of this technique can be seen in William James' foundational principle on which pragmatism is based. Taking his cue from the theme of the biblical writing of the apostle with the same last name, William twisted it to read, "Whatever works is true." The apostle had said, "Whatever is true will work." Notice the distortion and the profound difference?

A similar falsification has occurred with the concept of relativism. Relativism, properly defined, means that different ideas or things must be seen *in relationship* to each other and to some reference point. The pragmatists have altered this to mean that all ideas or things must be understood in relation to the human perceiver. They are thus humanists at heart, and man, for all humanists, is the measure or ultimate judge of all things. The pragmatists' position, therefore, is not true relativism, but humanistic subjectivism. And there lies a significant difference which should never ensnare the Christian.

Relativity cannot be equated with subjectivity. The idea of relativism should not be construed to mean that truth is subjective, although that is what is meant by the truth-denier who has succeeded in perverting our understanding. The meaning of "relativity" can easily be illustrated by reference to our own persons. I am a father, I am a son, I am an uncle, I am a brother. If you, the reader, are of the male sex, you can probably say the same things, all of them being true. If you are of the female sex, you will have to change your relative terms. We are all relatives, and we all have relatives, meaning simply that we stand not alone, but in organic relationship to other persons. With a certain measure of historical backtracking we are led to conclude that the whole human race is related through the historical Adam. This universal personal relationship, although frequently strained and often ignored, does not rile us. And neither should ideological relativity, for "All truth is relative" is merely a cogent way of stating that all truth must be seen and understood in its relationships.

The truths of American exploration and colonization, for example, cannot be apprehended apart from the objective historical realities of the Reformation and the Renaissance. Those historical truths must, in turn, be seen in the context of expanding European nationalism and the breakup of medieval feudalism. To ignore such relationships would be a mark of poor scholarship, but merely to push the relationships in a reverse chronological direction is also inadequate.

All truth is related, but just as in our personal, physical relationships, it must be related to something or someone, to an absolute, to a fixed, unchanging, yet always contemporary reference point. And what is that focal point for all our ideas and concepts? For the Christian the answer is disarmingly simple: It is "Christ Himself . . . the Creator who made everything in heaven and earth, the things we can see and the things we can't; the spirit world with its kings and kingdoms, its rulers and authorities: all were made by Christ for His own use and glory. He was before all else began and it is His power that holds everything together" (Col. 1:16-17). If anything is to be true, it must be *true to God*.

Truth, in all its ideological, personal, ethical and spiritual ramifications, is not a collection of independent elements, nor is it subject to flux and situational gyrations. On the contrary, it is fixed and absolute, no matter what the pragmatists may claim. Take, for example, the proposition expressed in Question 8 of our opening quiz. It was most definitely the Wednesday afternoon of July 9 when the quiz was constructed. Unstated, but assumed by the person making the statement, was the fact that it was composed in the Pacific Time Zone, at which time it was 2:00 P.M., daylight savings time.

We deal in assumptions such as the above with a great deal of regularity and think nothing of it. Certain understood elements are casually accepted or assumed by both the speaker and the listener. When those understood elements are also included in our meaning, we have a true statement whose truth will not change. The original statement will thus always be true, no matter who perceives it or under what circumstances it is heard. It is a fact whose truth is fixed for all eternity. What is true today will also be true tomorrow and next year and next century. Truth does not change, even though our conception of it and our relationship to it may fluctuate wildly. But thanks be to God, those who are maturing in faith and becoming one with Christ no longer sway to and fro with every wind of doctrine.

To determine that truth is fixed and firm and not subject to human interpretation is to refute the pragmatic claim that there are no absolutes. The pragmatic claim can also be rejected by appeal to the principle of internal consistency. For example, whenever the subjective humanists claim that "there are no absolutes," they make their assertion as an absolute statement which is always true and tolerates no exceptions. If there are *no* absolutes, then their own statement could not be absolute and must therefore be true only part of the time. The pragmatists prefer, though, to allow for at least one exception, namely, the absoluteness of their own statement, which they hope the reader will not detect. As soon as one exception is found, of course, their whole assertion is exposed as false.

A second way in which the pragmatists formulate their argument is to say that "nothing is fixed, for everything is constantly changing." If *every*thing were changing, as they assert, then change itself would be a *constant*, which fact they ignorantly delight in expressing. "Constant change," furthermore, is a contradiction in terms which renders their entire argument suspect. As soon as one constant can be identified, the pragmatists are forced to admit that some, but not all, things change and that some things are fixed and therefore absolute. Once that point is reached, the Christian has a beautiful opportunity to identify those things which are the same for all eternity, beginning, of course, with God.

Discussion

1. Should true and false tests be used in our schools? If so, what precautions must be followed when constructing and administering them?

2. Should Christians categorically reject all that non-Christians have written? Should we allow obviously non-Christian writings to be studied by our students?

3. How can one best illustrate the total interrelatedness of "truths," "true conduct" and Christ the Truth?

4. Why is it that Christians so often cry out against "relativism"? Does that kind of appeal help or hinder the Christian faith?

5. What is meant by an "integrated curriculum"? If one did not see God as the reference point or fixed source of all knowledge, what other options would he have for a reference point?

VI

How Does One View the Child?

I know a few teachers who talk and act as if their student charges were all angels, just waiting to sprout wings. Their talk is a bit unrealistic and occasionally borders on the nauseating. The students, they contend, are so good, so anxious to learn, and so polite to everyone else in the classroom. To punish them or to accuse them of wrongdoing would be unthinkable.

There are other teachers who consider it their prime duty each day to tame the little devils who have been assigned to their room. Kids, they say, are not to be trusted for one minute, for they will steal, cheat and destroy the classroom furniture as soon as you turn your back on them. Such teachers' language is not very pleasant, either, and may even border on the vulgar or inhumane. If their judgment were followed, the only teachers who could survive in the blackboard jungle are ones with skin as thick as elephants', eyes on four sides of the head, hearts as cold as a ship's anchor, and the approach to life of a big-city policeman.

These two types of teachers represent extremes, to be sure, but they are not uncommon in our nation's schools. Both types lack a sanctified common sense and constitute a real hazard to any level-headed administrator, with their real weakness not easily corrected. Their prime deficiency is that they fail to possess a thorough and accurate understanding of the child, holding instead to a warped and distorted view which has probably been allowed to crystalize through the long period of their own growing up.

The ideas about the child that are perpetuated in college and university education and psychology courses should be cause for concern to every committed Christian, for it is here that many teachers develop their professional attitudes toward students. The false impressions that may have been allowed to grow during their more formative years are cemented there with the official blessing and assumed expertise of those whose deepest insights have come from reading Aristotle, Sigmund Freud, John Dewey, or B. F. Skinner. For, whether we like to admit it or not, these men and others like them have had a profound impact on our way of thinking and our views about the nature of man.

Some Views to Be Considered

The Psalmist David asked already long before the time of Christ, "What is man, that thou are mindful of him?" That question is still one of the most important that can be asked of and by those who are called to be teachers. What is man?

Although each professor in our schools of teacher training has his own preferred view which he transmits with varying degrees of commitment, it is our purpose here to cite very briefly some of the major ideas which have affected education in our culture. These views are presented in their most abbreviated, capsulized forms. To understand and assess them in all their complexity, the reader will have to find the original discourses or rely on some secondary source whose primary business it is to expound these ideas in great detail.

One of Plato's main ideas about the essential nature of man is that man is born with innate ideas. Expressing his views primarily through the speeches of Socrates, Plato argued that the child was born with innate knowledge, already at birth in possession of all ideas. The purpose of teaching, therefore, was "to lead out" (*educere*) the student by appropriate questioning, the technique since known as the Socratic method. The teacher, said Socrates, was a midwife.

Aristotle, who was a disciple of Plato, held to many of his mentor's ideas, but with some notable variations. Aristotle, for instance, made a distinction between actuality and potentiality, insisting that the person held the *potential* for complete knowledge, but did not actually possess all ideas innately at birth. More importantly, though, Aristotle advanced a basically evolutionary view of man which was to come to fuller, clearer expression much later in the work of Charles Darwin. Asserting that there were various categories or levels of development, Aristotle placed man at the pinnacle of that development and referred to him as an animal possessing reason. Man, for Aristotle, was essentially a rational animal.

During the first part of the eighteenth century there arose a number of psychologist-philosophers who were variously labelled as realists or empiricists. Chief among them was John Locke who advocated a position diametrically opposed to that of Plato and Socrates. Man came into the world, said Locke, as a blank sheet or a "tabula rasa," possessing no innate ideas. In sharp contrast with the Platonic school of thought, Locke posited an empty mind which could only be filled as ideas came to the person, through sensory experiences, from the outside. Instead of emptying the mind and bringing to fruition that which was already there in germinal form, man was, like an empty bucket, to be filled. The teacher's primary task was, therefore, to impart knowledge and to disseminate information. This view is still the most prevalent in traditional schools and measures success by quantitative analysis of the facts and ideas assimilated. Conversely, the one who has absorbed *the most is the best* educated.

Karl Marx has pushed another view of man into the Western mentality, but his views have usually conflicted with the ideas of both the Platonists and the sensory empiricists. The essential, distinguishing trait of man, according to Marx, is that man is the only animal which has learned to master tools and is thus capable of controlling the economy. Man's tool-using abilities are crucial to the type of economic order that Marx envisioned, and thus are also of paramount importance in the learning process. Since the child is essentially an economic creature, it is crucial that he learn to use various tools velop marketable skills so that he can contribute to the economic good of the state. This vocational emphasis has frequently run contrary to the liberal arts idea which put book learning on a pedestal.

During the era of the democratic revolutions, another view of man was often expressed by the leaders of those movements. Man, they said, was master of his own destiny and was not to be ruled without his prior consent. Persons like Paine, Jefferson, Franklin, and Jackson expressed a briny irreverance toward their deistic, clock-maker God and claimed that man was possessed of certain natural, inalienable rights with which no man might meddle. Natural man, they said, was an autonomous political creature whose first business it was to serve his own interests.

In our own twentieth century, one of the outstanding molders of public opinion was John Dewey. Standing not alone, but in full consort with persons of a pragmatic, empirical, and progressive bent, Dewey perpetrated numerous ideas about the nature of man. Central among those was the concept that man was *a social resultant*, completely the product of his collective experiences. Man was whatever he became, affected and influenced by his parents, his peers, his schools, his communities, and his churches. Always evolving in evolutionary fashion, man had the potential to select his influences so as to become perfect and create for himself the perfect society. Far from original, Dewey borrowed selectively from his predecessors so long as their views harmonized with his own subjective position.

Other major personalities also contributed significantly to the Western mind. Among them we could include Descartes, Rousseau, Darwin, Emerson, Thorndike, Skinner, and now Piaget. Each of these has added significantly to the increasingly complex picture of human understanding. If the student finds in any one or any combination of them his primary source for understanding the child, he will have joined the majority of teachers who have chosen to view God's most precious creatures without relationship to the God who created them and whose they are. All of the foregoing, in

58

spite of their occasional allusions to a mystical deity, are secularists. Devoid of divine light, the intellectual giants are analagous to those blind men of Indostan, to learning much inclined, but always missing the mark.

What Does the Christian Believe?

While not ignoring the collective insights of the worldly sages, the Christian nevertheless starts his search in another place. Knowing that God's Word is the only authoritative guide for all of life, and thus for his view of man, the Christian turns first of all to God Himself for insight and analysis concerning the crowning creature of God's creation. Knowing, too, that one's view of the student is the most important factor in determining teachers' conduct and attitudes, the Christian will pursue this search of Scripture with all diligence, asking daily for the enlightenment which only the Holy Spirit can give.

In the twentieth century world which seems at times to be completely controlled by secular thought, the Christian must be open to the fact that religious ideas and terminology exist not in isolated compartments and sovereign spheres, but are full of relevance of pedagogical concerns. Those terms and concepts, so faithfully taught in weekly sermons and catechism classes, are potent with meaning for that teacher who confronts children five days a week in the formal school. Equipped with the religious vision which only Christianity has to offer, those children will be other than rational animals, empty buckets, and environmental products. They will be more than budding angels or frustrating little demons, although those, too, are religious expressions. Fully understood, those little and not so little people who populate our classrooms will be a fantastic array of character and quality, all related to the God without whom they could not exist. In the pages that follow, some of those qualities will be briefly explained, but before we embark on that, certain qualifications must be laid down.

When talking about the nature of the student, we must remember that we can talk in either a general or a specific sense. Speaking specifically, we are concerned about the character or quality of individual students in contrast with other individuals. We can say, for instance, that Student A is reticent, dishonest, kind to animals, fuzzy-cheeked, tall and afraid of the opposite sex. Another student might be boisterous, hyper-kinetic, affectionate, slow to learn, and polite to teachers. This kind of analysis is crucial to good teaching, but it is an endless process, for every child has unique, personal characteristics which set him apart from all his neighbors. Although education departments must encourage the careful observation of these personal traits, this work must never overshadow the analysis of those characteristics common to all men, for it is the general rather than the specific view which determines pedagogical posture.

A *second* factor which directs the Christian's attempt to understand man is that involving man's overall relationship to God. When Scripture is studied, there are three distinct "states" or conditions in which man can be found. If one were to focus exclusively on the first part of Genesis, as Rousseau so erroneously did, man would have to be judged perfect, or at least very good, for he existed then in the pre-fallen or prelapsarian state. True, man was originally good, perfectly free, wholly knowing, and joyfully obedient in his service to God, but that condition only lasted a short time. Since Adam, all have sinned and lived in disobedience, thus outlining for the Christian the fallen, the unregenerate, or the postlapsarian state. Some religious groups who operate schools have never been able to see beyond this state and have made "the saving of souls" the primary business of the classroom, punctuating the daily lesson with modified altar calls and gearing their admission policies to a proselytizing purpose.

Admittedly there are thousands and even millions of unregenerate persons in the world who need to experience the saving power of Christ, but to view all children as being so positioned is to do God a great injustice. The *third* state, and that which is most significant for parentally-controlled Christian schools, is that in which man is said to be already saved

60

or regenerated by the electing love of God. It is only in this state that one can talk about the "covenant" or agreement which God has made with believers *and their children.* Because the parentally-controlled Christian schools are really voluntary organizations designed by parents to train up their children in the way which God has prescribed for them, many, if not most, of their students can be assumed to exist within the regenerate state. Not perfected certainly, but at least beginning that long, arduous and hazard-strewn road of sanctification. The teacher, then, who looks at his students as already angels or still devils does not belong in a Christian school, for his views are out of harmony with the Christian perspective.

Assuming, then, that all students are either in state two or three, what concrete traits or characteristics can be adduced so as to portray a meaningful and significant picture for the classroom teacher? In order to answer that question, let us move from the ordinary and expected to those characteristics which are often ignored, or, to put it differently, from the known to the unusual.

First, all men, including children of kindergarten, junior high, and college age, are sinners. All children are inclined *by nature* to hate their bus driver, their teacher, their classmates, and even their brothers or sisters. Not all at the same time, certainly, and not even all the time, but *the inclination* is there for all to see. Listen to them talk sometimes; watch how they tease their peers. Let their parents give them a measure of support and see how they can crucify the best of teachers. Sinners, disobedient, prone toward mischief, living in violation of God's laws, certainly yes, but that is not the whole picture, for if it were, no self-respecting teacher would want to make his living in the classroom.

Second, and closely related to the first, is the characteristic of *total depravity.* Since that trait has been more often misunderstood than not, it needs some explanation. Total depravity, when properly defined, means that the person is imperfect in every facet of his being. Because of the effects of sin, he is no longer perfect as God originally created him, but is now imperfect in his thinking, his feeling, his memorizing, his loving, his reasoning, and every other way that can be imagined. The perfectionist, then, who wants all his efforts to be without flaw is thus doomed to a life of perpetual frustration. The teacher, too, who demands perfect work from all his students will be needlessly harsh and lacks the good sense which only a realistic Christian possesses.

The most common misconception about this trait is that which identifies total depravity with *absolute* depravity, which is hardly a biblical position. Absolute depravity holds that all good was eradicated from man as a consequence of Adam's sin and that nothing good can ever come from man again. The teacher who views his students as a collection of little devils probably has made this error somewhere in his developmental years. Although some students would almost convince you that absolute depravity is real in their exceptional case, the Christian will find little in Scripture to substantiate this view.

A *third* characteristic of the child is that he is a disciple. Because of secular influences in our society, we tend to think of discipleship in a very limited way, with the only real disciples those twelve men who followed Jesus on His earthly ministry. But every student in every classroom is a disciple, for the word is synonymous with learner or student. The word is derived from two latin words, *discere* and *discipulus.* In the noun form, the word means one who receives instruction from another, thus referring to pupils, scholars, or students. Matthew, Peter, James, John, et.al. walked and talked with Jesus, thus earning for themselves the appellation as students of the only perfect teacher and therefore as models for discipleship. The verb form *discere* means to teach or to train and applies to the work of the teacher, making it wholly legitimate to think of the teacher as discipling his disciples.

If you think of your students as disciples, you will likely be abnormal in your description, but you will also be fully accurate. Such a view of teaching should prove cause for deep reflection, however, for Jesus Himself warned that whoever would lead a little one astray, it were better that a millstone be hanged around his neck and he be cast into the sea to drown.

In Reformed theology there is another pair of terms which is frequently applied to man. Those terms are *prophet* and *priest*. During the Old Testament times of Elijah and Elisha there were "schools of the prophets" at which young persons, usually boys, learned to become prophets. Then as now, there were false schools as well as ones that proclaimed the truth. Both terms, however, have so fallen under a shroud of mysticism that we think of them as some sort of strange workers of magic or future predictors. Again it must be seen that the descriptions are still relevant for today's world if properly defined. The prophet of old was not a predictor of the future, but merely one who proclaimed the messages that God wanted His people to hear. Since God knew the future as well as the past, he specially informed certain of His prophets what would happen, instructing them to spread the message as a warning to His people.

God calls every Christian to proclaim His message of justice and salvation, thereby making every one of us His prophets. Not many will rise to the prominence of an Elijah or Jeremiah, and not all of us do our proclaiming with a full measure of obedience, but prophets we are nonetheless.

A cardinal truth of Christianity rejuvenated by Martin Luther but still stymied by the church of Rome is the universal priesthood of all believers. Every child is a priest, both permitted and instructed to come directly into God's presence through prayer and to make intercession for his family's and neighbors' needs. The child must learn to pray, just as he must learn to read, to sing, to drive a car, and to respect authority. The teacher in the classroom, either by example or by organized and conscious instruction, is always developing the life and work of those young priests (and priestesses). The Christian teacher who does not or may not pray in the classroom is also teaching the child, either that prayer is not important or only to be done outside the school. No matter which, how much better it would be if the teacher daily taught her students how to pray and what to pray.

63

Prophets, priests, disciples, and sinners, all sitting there in a literature lesson or learning how to divide with double digits! Prophets learning how to proclaim the truth of God by practicing the skills of reading, speaking, singing, and composition. Disciples learning to follow the way of righteousness rather than madly pursuing the pleasures of sin for a season. That is the way a Christian teacher views his pupils! But that is not all, for the Christian perspective is more complete and more complex than anything offered by the worldly wise.

A student is also a *believer*. But is that true only for those who have been saved by grace and brought into the regenerate state? When casually used, the word believer is used to describe Christians in contrast with non-Christians, who are the unbelievers. Such usage is not forbidden, for the Bible uses the same meanings and descriptions. But there is another, expanded meaning which is freighted with significance for every classroom. Let me illustrate. Just recently there was a sixth grade boy and his parents in my office, wanting to consider the option of transferring from a state school to our Christian institution. In explaining some of our differences, we touched on the matter of evolution versus creation. When I pointed out that our teachers held to the creationist position, the little boy vigorously shook his head in disbelief. Through the work of his teachers, and in spite of his parents, he had come to believe that the evolutionary explanation was true and the biblical position was false.

A believer is any one who believes an idea or position to be true, while an unbeliever is one who holds it to be false. In conventional Christian parlance, the believer is he who accepts the gospel as truth. If extended beyond that narrow definition, however, each of us is both believer and unbeliever, for we are always believing something to be true and its negation to be false. When I accept the Genesis account of creation as a true explanation, I am a believer, but then, if I am to be consistent, I must also believe the Darwinian explanation to be false, making me simultaneously a believer and an unbeliever.

The teacher who has a low credibility rating with his

students is frequently a hazard to them, for they know not when to believe and when to disbelieve. This struck home to me in my first year of teaching when I assumed it wise to point out a few factual errors in the history textbook. Whom should my students believe: Some wise young product fresh out of graduate school or a textbook? Many of the students knew immediately which to believe and consequently listened incredulously for weeks to come. Such choices are not unusual in the classroom, even though many of our schools persist in perpetuating the mistaken notion that textbooks are flawless and their authors infallible. But such should not continue, for there is only one book that is perfect and only one infallible author. The Christian knows which that is.

We have only touched briefly on the qualities of man that are biblically sanctioned. To be exhaustive would require more than double the space here allotted, but one point should be clear. The biblical view of man, which we so easily confine to a narrow sphere of theological parlance, is quite different from that offered by the conventional psychologists and philosophers whose views have dominated teachers' preparation courses. In spite of those differences, and maybe because of them, the Christian view of the student is not without pedagogical relevance. To see one's students as sinners and saints, as prophets and priests, as disciples and as believers, that is to catch a glimpse of their real worth and importance. Created in the image of God, the child is more than a rational animal and a product of his environment. He is the crown of God's creation, fearfully and wonderfully made, and so beautifully complex as to enliven the thoughts of even the most brilliant teacher as he seeks to understand him.

Discussion

1. How can a teacher improve his credibility rating, so that students will more quickly accept his explanations as truth? What factors will erode a credibility rating?

2. Comparing Plato's idea of innate knowledge with Locke's tabula rasa, which position, if either, is in harmony with Scripture? What should be a thoroughly biblical position?

3. What profit is there in studying the writings of such men as Aristotle, Descartes, Dewey, or Skinner? What dangers are there?

4. Remembering the definitions of truth and falsehood from Chapter IV, can it be said that all non-Christian views of man are false? Are there degrees of falsehood?

5. What other terms or descriptions from Scripture can be applied to the contemporary student so as to complete the picture? How is each of these to be translated from theological to pedagogical language?

6. Would it be biblically defensible to describe the child as a sexual being? A chemical being? An electrical creature? Why or why not?

VII

Which Educational Objectives Are Most Valuable?

For two years my wife and I found it necessary to place our children in a public school. Though all our family experiences had centered in Christian schools, circumstances placed us in a community where there was no Christian school. This new experience was good for all of us, not because the education was so excellent, but because we had opportunity to learn first-hand, something of the character of public schools in America.

Despite the legal restrictions and the presumed "wall of separation" between religion and education, our two younger children had fine Christian teachers whose values and perspective we could share. Our eldest son, though, was in junior high school and had a quite different set of circumstances. One of his teachers was the most rabid evolutionist we had ever encountered. Another was a rock music nut who specialized in the off-beat. Other faculty members represented middle-class, secular American values. The principal saw his role as the great pacifier, trying to please everyone so that each person could exercise his libertarian options and have his own way.

In such situations the child, and especially the adolescent, can easily be pulled mentally asunder and lose direction or purpose for life. The majority of students in that school gave the impression that they were confused, mixed-up kids who didn't know what they believed or where they were going. Like blind sheep, they passionately followed the person, whether that was teacher or peer, who sounded most convincing and sincere at the moment.

Robert Ulich, the noted educational analyst, recently condemned American schools when he wrote,

> Looking back at education as it has been during the past decades and as it is still today in many places, one discovers a frantic emphasis on science, but at the same time a frightening lack of truly human purpose. Apparently education has alienated itself from the perennial concerns of mankind (*Education in Western Culture*, p. 127).

One does not have to look far in America's public schools to find the scenes about which Ulich was writing. Regrettably, the same conditions often are true for Christian schools as well, for they sometimes lose their way, too, and seem to run off in a multitude of directions at once. Far too often the lament is heard that people do not know why Christian schools exist or what they are trying to accomplish.

Christian schools ought to be characterized by the fact that they know where they are going and what they are trying to do. Their goals ought to be clearly stated, stable, and pointing consistently in the same direction. Unlike the public schools, their aim ought not to shift with every new wind of educational doctrine. Unless it becomes obvious that they have been headed in the wrong direction, they should not change course often.

In public education today there seems to be a great deal of confusion and aimless wandering. Such should not deter or distract the Christian, however. The apostle Paul, in his letter to the Philippians, reminds us that we should be like the runner in a race who looks straight ahead and keeps his eyes fixed on the goal that is set before him. Remembering that principle, we should not turn our direction to the public schools, to see what they are doing, but we should focus our eyes in God's holy Word, to see what kind of goal or what sets of objectives He has spelled out for us. If Scripture is truly to be our only authoritative guide for all of life, then, logically and consistently, it must also be our guide or direction-finder for educational objectives and purpose.

But that task is no simple one. The Christian can be full of good intentions and can earnestly search the Scriptures, but can and often will miss the mark. Rena Foy, in a burst of candor once said, "Of all the questions confronting educators those pertaining to the aims of education are the most difficult to answer; they are the most complicated, the most penetrating" (*The World of Education*, p. 5). Whoever has tried to articulate clearly and precisely what the school should be doing can sympathize with Foy, because the aims of education, whether for an individual or for society at large, are extremely difficult to define. "What may begin as a relatively simple discussion regarding what should be studied, or what should be taught, has a way of developing into a consideration of mankind's deepest and most vital values" (*ibid.*, p. 4).

Merely knowing that the Bible contains the answers we seek does not automatically guarantee that we will find those answers. Like the vast majority of educators today, we do not know how to proceed or what precisely it is for which we should look. If we state the problem or phrase the question badly, we may look for years and never find the answers. For example, we could ask the question in any of the following forms:

1. *What is our school's educational objective?* Phrased this way, we might turn for answer to Proverbs 22:6: "Train up a child in the way he should go, and when he is old he will not depart from it." That answer has been a guiding light for Christian educators for decades and even centuries, but it is hardly exhaustive in meaning and fails to shed light on such legitimate questions as to whether we should study modern math or traditional arithmetic. It would be easy, certainly, if God had set aside one chapter or book in which He clearly spelled out all the educational objectives for twentieth century schools, but He has seen fit not to fragment the gospel in that way.

2. *What are you trying to accomplish?* Such a phrasing of the question legitimately focuses on educational goals, but it assumes that the source of answers lies with the teacher. Such a question compels introspection and self-examination,

worthwhile activities in themselves, but is hardly productive of those answers which can transcend individual human weakness.

3. *What should our teachers teach*? At the high school and college levels, this is the most common form of question used to unravel the riddle of educational objectives. Because it is so common, it is necessary to call special attention to the way in which it is answered.

When confronted with the above question, most teachers beyond the elementary level would respond by saying that they should be teaching the subjects in which they majored or specialized at college or graduate school. In spite of their enthusiasm, it is philosophically ridiculous to say that we should teach math or history or biology or music. It would make just as much sense for a farmer to say that he was trying to raise corn planters or produce tractors. It would make as much sense to say that carpenters are trying to build hammers, saws, and nails.

Obviously the above statements do not make much sense, yet many of our supposedly best educators are often confused to the point where they do not know what they are talking about. They have become so subject-centered that they have lost clarity of vision and long-range perspective.

Why do we not say that a farmer should produce tractors? Or a carpenter build hammers? Or a teacher teach history? Because the tractor and the hammer and the history are *tools* with which to produce something else. They are the *means*, the *implements*, and not the *ends* or *objectives*. Yet teachers everywhere have an uncanny knack for avoiding the questions of purpose and are turning instead to questions of means or methodology. If a carpenter spent his best energy analyzing his tools and never setting his sights on the cabinet or house to be constructed, we would soon dismiss him from the job. When teachers do that, however, we honor them with a promotion and call them professor.

Properly Phrasing the Problem

If we are to find the answers to the questions of purpose, we need to avoid the pitfalls of badly phrased questions. We need to turn our attention temporarily away from the subjects of curriculum and also the teachers. That is not to say that curriculum and teachers are unimportant. Nothing could be further from the truth, but turning our attention in another direction is necessary if we are to avoid the fallacies of both the subject-centered and the teacher-centered schools.

The proper focus for determining correct and clear objectives is the child or student who must acquire the learnings. We need to ask: What must the child learn? Refreshing our memory from previous chapters, we need to remember that the human being is called by God to undergo change or transformation (cf. Rom. 12:1-3). Through the sanctifying power of the Holy Spirit, we need to be transformed from what *is* to what *ought*, from the undesirable *present* to the desired *future*, from what we *are* to what we *should become.*

This required transformation becomes most apparent when we observe and analyze our youth. In the following illustration, note the obvious changes which are clearly implied if a child is to progress from *Being* to *Becoming*:

Being	Becoming	Needs to Learn
non-reader	reader	to read
immature	mature	to accept and handle responsibility
awkward	coordinated	to control muscles
poor speller	good speller	to spell words
scribbler	neat writer	to write legibly
disobedient	obedient	to obey
ignorant	knowledgable	to know the truth
monotone	a singer	to read musical scales

Learning and teaching, when so perceived, are essentially aimed at an explanatory of changes which are occurring or need to occur in the learner. Such an approach, in contrast with the others suggested on preceding pages, helps us to see objectives most clearly, for it focuses directly on the learnings to be acquired and not on the persons or means responsible for producing those learnings. But here, too, is a pitfall, for it would be easy to slide into the errors of child-centeredness. John Dewey teetered precariously on the brink of that fallacy during most of his professional career. Countless educators in the twentieth century have wholly succumbed to this point of view, ascribing to the child a mild form of deity and boldly proclaiming that their curricula are truly child-centered.

The Christian needs to avoid that stance, for he should be neither subject-centered nor child-centered. The Christian, by contrast, is always *God-centered*, recognizing that in Christ all things cohere and in relationship to Him must all things be understood. The temporary focusing on the child, then, is not inconsistent with such God-centeredness, for the child is first of all a creature of God, commanded to love and serve the Master whose he is. Since the child belongs to God, it is God who has the first say in what the child should learn. Through His written Word, God spells out in unmistakable language what we need to learn and what kind of persons we should become. As long as we keep that fact in the forefront of our minds, we can safely proceed to repeat the question: What *should* the student learn?

What Should the Student Learn?

When questions about educational objectives or goals are seriously asked, a variety of answers are usually forthcoming. In some cases the answers are so prolific, that the respondent soon finds it necessary to divert his attention to the matter of taxonomy or categories of answers. If, for example, fifty or a hundred answers were given, some grouping would have to occur. The most common taxonomy used today is that advanced by the secularists Bloom and Krothwal and found in most secular textbooks. In its essential form, the categories are cognitive, affective, and psycho-motor. The cognitive is best translated as intellectual or academic, the affective as personal or emotional, and the psycho-motor as physical.

This taxonomy is uncritically accepted by thousands of schoolmen, and has even been refined in an attempt to delineate minute concerns, but it fails miserably when confronted with basic and simple problems. For example, would learning *to sing* be classified as intellectual, personal, or physical? Obviously the physical body is involved in such learning activity, for one could not sing without exercising and controlling the vocal chords, not to mention the eyes, the diaphragm, the mouth, the lungs, the ears, and a great many lesser parts. So, too, the affective area, for singing is clearly an emotional or personal expression, conveying attitudes and feelings on every score. Not to slight the musician, we must also recognize that the mind or intellect is clearly involved. Not all narrow-minded spokesmen for the academic departments would quietly concur, but the point should require no further demonstration.

The same type of problem occurs if we try to fit such learnings as typing, writing, or spelling into Bloom and Krothwal's taxonomy. In such and every other learning activity, the total person is involved, not just his fingers or his voice box or his brain. The whole organic person learns, with every part of the person involved in every learning. To argue otherwise is both to fragment the person into disjointed parts and to reduce a total learning experience to its most visible component.

In an attempt to separate itself from the contemporary secular mold, the National Union of Christian Schools some years ago commissioned its resident educational philosopher to draft a new taxonomy for learning goals. The finished and accepted product bore a fresh configuration, composed now of Intellectual, Moral-Decisional, and Creative categories. The external break with secular thought was obvious, but the internal weaknesses were identical. By testing this taxonomy against such legitimate goals as learning to sing, to read, to type, to pray, or to write, one finds again that the objectives encompass all three categories, with none claiming exclusive right. Again, this taxonomy, devised for the NUCS by Beversluis, does violence to the wholeness of man and attempts to divorce the singing voice not only from the imagination, but also from the obedient heart and the ever operative mind.

Given a simple choice, Beversluis would be hard-pressed to choose the category for any of the above goals.

The key to effective taxonomy lies not in disjointing the learner, but in seeing clearly the relationship between taxonomy and axiology, which is merely the study of *values*. Certainly educational objectives must be categorized, for large, unruly numbers of objectives can be identified as legitimate. What must be emphasized though, is that not all objectives are equally important or valuable. Some must be of great value, while others must be of less or minimal value.

Try the following exercise and then compare your results with those of other persons.

OBJECTIVES AND VALUES

Rate the following educational objectives according to their importance or relative value. Rate the most important as 1 and the least important as 4. Those which you consider to be false or illegitimate objectives, rate as "x". Rate all the others as 1, 2, 3, or 4. There is no specific distribution of numbers.

Children need to learn:

_____ to spell correctly
_____ to read rapidly
_____ to read critically
_____ to discern between truth and falsehood
_____ to write legibly

_____ to share toys and materials
_____ to dress themselves
_____ to wash their hands
_____ to sing
_____ to pray

_____ the difference between male and female
_____ to subtract
_____ to add
_____ to tell time
_____ to obey bicycle and traffic safety rules

_____ to obey their parents and teachers
_____ to love their neighbor (classmates, family, friends)
_____ to appreciate the beauty of creation
_____ to hit a softball
_____ to ride a bicycle

_____ how other people live in the world
_____ topographical features of their own country
_____ to play a musical instrument
_____ to sing in tune
_____ to discern between good and bad TV programs

Would your answers differ from those of a non-Christian? If God saw fit to again become incarnate, would your answers bear close resemblance to His? Would the answers given by Christian teachers differ significantly from those given by non-Christian teachers?

Whether we are conscious of it or not, every school system and every individual has and puts on display a value structure. We all have ranked values which come to expression in various ways. A school's catalog of courses, for example, will tell the observer which courses are most important. Those courses that are compulsory and required of every student are clearly construed to be of higher value than those which are offered only occasionally or on an optional basis. Those courses which are given large blocks of time in the schedule also give clues to the same issue. Classroom teachers, too, put their values on display in numerous ways, as do the students, who either accept or reject those values.

Most important, however, is the fact that God has priorities and values which take precedence over ours. Although John Dewey and other subjectivists were never inclined to concur, God has a set of absolute, eternal values which are clearly spelled out in Scripture. When God the Holy Spirit inspired men to write the books of the Bible, He could have filled the pages with countless different concerns and issues, but He chose the ones He did as an expression of that which is and was most important. "Seek ye first the Kingdom . . . and all these others things will be added" is one of the clearest and most cogent expressions, but that is only one of many. Another that deserves serious attention commands us to think on those things that are pure, lovely, and of good report.

One of the greatest and most significant differences between Christian schools and public schools is the difference between values. This fact became obvious to the author on different occasions when he had opportunity to present the foregoing list of objectives to both Christian and non-Christian faculty groups. The results and the accompanying attitudes were so clearly different that one need never doubt again that there is a distinctive difference.

Questions to ponder:
1. Is "value" first of all a noun or a verb? How would a Christian answer? How would a non-Christian? What are the implications of each position?
2. Are human values affected by ethnic, racial, or cultural backgrounds? If so, how can one argue that values are absolute?
3. Can you "test" to determine whether our children have learned "to love their neighbor" or "to appreciate poetry"?
4. How *do* we resolve differences of values? How *should* we?
5. What criteria should we set up for categorizing values as primary (1), secondary (2), tertiary (3) or incidental (4)?
6. Does the author's taxonomy, as suggested in question 5 above, overcome the objections raised against the taxonomies of Bloom and Beversluis? Does it raise new problems?
7. Do you think that God would approve and endorse the priorities or values of your school? Or are we inclined to major in the minors and minor in the majors?

VIII

What Is the Curriculum?

In the previous chapter we made some slightly disparaging remarks about the subjects taught in the schools. No doubt some persons who teach at the secondary or college levels have taken issue with that relatively low assessment, in spite of the obvious claim that subjects are a necessary ingredient in the schooling process.

If we are to avoid the fallacy of subject-centeredness, which, incidentally, countless educators see not as error, but as the only viable position, then we must see clearly what the curriculum is, and what it is not. First of all, we must not confuse the curriculum with the ends or objectives of education. As pointed out previously in our discussion about farmers, carpenters, and teachers, the subject is the *means* and not the end of teaching. Contrary to popular expression, we do not teach reading, history, science or music. No, we teach children to read, to understand the past, to do various experiments, and to appreciate one form of music over another. That is *what* we do, but we must also ask *how* we do that.

We achieve the above objectives *by means of* organized collections of ideas, information, or activities. The subjects, then, are the means or tools or instruments by which we attempt to accomplish that which we have previously judged to be worth doing. If we are in control of the educational process, and not mere slaves to some unknown textbook publishers, then we will choose our courses and materials carefully so as to reach our pre-determined goals most efficiently. The opposite, and too frequent, pattern emerges when teachers slavishly attempt to get through a textbook and then pray that some good results will mystically occur.

But the curriculum is more than a means to a set of pre-scribed ends. It is also, by common agreement, a catalog of courses offered by a school, whether that be a law school, a Sunday school, or the local elementary school where all the neighborhood kids congregate five days a week. The mere catalog of courses, though, is nothing more than a skeletal outline of the curriculum. Simply to name such terms as geography, speech, algebra or arithmetic is to be less than descriptive or precise. What is all included in that geography class? What kinds of activities and explanations does that entail? I knew too well one so-called instructor in geography who never got beyond a daily eulogizing of the evolutionary themes and their various proponents. In that case the curriculum became a serious, semester-long attempt to convert the students to an evolutionary mentality. All the pictures, the audio-visual displays, the student-teacher arguments, the tests, the jokes, and the reading assignments were part of that curriculum. Such is always the case. Not only the course titles, but the entire contents of those courses constitute the curriculum.

When viewed this way, it becomes apparent that the class-room teacher, and not the administrator or the Board of Directors, is the prime determiner of a school's curriculum. Teachers, then, should reflect seriously before they cry out for more involvement in curriculum planning. When compared with those who merely name the courses to be included in the catalog, teachers have the greater opportunity and the greater burden of responsibility.

A third definition of the curriculum is one that most analysts have overlooked. Most succinctly stated, the curriculum is a selective sampling of the *past* used in the *present* for the sake of the *future*. It is a selective sampling because only a tiny fragment of what has occurred or is understood can be utilized. Even the most advanced graduate course in history, complete with the often unattainable reading assignments, touches only a small, select segment of that data that could have been recorded or martialled for use. More surprising, however, is the fact that the curriculum is always *past*, and not present or future. It may be the ancient past, the not too distant past, or even the immediate past, but it is past nonetheless, for the present is but a fleeting moment and the future is not yet. What happened yesterday or last week or even this morning is now history. It can be recalled, reviewed, and even re-enacted, but it cannot be redone. In recall and review we can put it to use for a menagerie of purposes, but whenever we use it, it will be in the present, for that is when all of us live.

We use the past in the present, not for the past or the present, but for the future. We impart an historical event in order that tomorrow and next year and in adulthood our charges can enjoy more enlightened understanding and make more accurate, intelligent decisions. We instruct a teenager to drive defensively so that the next time he or she goes out with the car an accident may be prevented. Unlike the existentialist, the Christian lives not for the present moment, but for the future, so that he might develop into that mature manhood and Christ-like mentality of which the Scriptures speak. But in living for the future, he does not ignore the past or deny the present. He cannot, for they are part of God's total revelation, to which he must respond. That which has been learned and been recorded by someone else or has occurred before must be used now in order that tomorrow we can handle more responsibly the blessings and challenges we each receive.

The curriculum has also been characterized by some astute analysts as windows, clear and unobstructed, through which we can peer into the world all around us. Chemistry, thus, is a glimpse at that aspect of reality which is not only in the laboratory or pharmacy, but also in the kitchen cabinet and the pool in which we swim. History, too, is a window into the past, not offering unlimited vision, but a pointed, one-direction look at what has occurred before.

79

Windows, as usual, are means by which to look through walls, not objects to be studied for their own sake. The walls are of sundry types, sometimes of wood and stone, but often, too, they are cultural and psychological. When the windows are clear and unobstructed by egocentric teachers, grand and marvelous panoramas can be opened to students, giving them a fleeting glimpse of that omniscience which only God possesses.

But there is still another meaning of curriculum which needs to be examined. For those who are etymological buffs, always clamoring for the derivation of a word, there is a special treat in store here. "Curriculum" is an old Latin word, a noun meaning running, a race course, or a chariot. Such may seem far-fetched, but further examination reveals that the Latin word *curricle* (n.) meant a two-wheeled chaise drawn by two horses abreast. This concept of a race is further supported by the word *currere*, a verb form, meaning to run. Near the end of a semester or quarter at school, many students would be easily convinced that the curriculum is truly a race course, on which they are being helplessly careened toward a collision with the final exam. Their suspicions, we would assert, are not far from the mark if we could recall the acceleration quality discussed earlier.

The curriculum is not exactly a race course, but it is certainly an accelerated experience designed to speed up the learning process. In chemical terminology, it is a catalyst, purposely employed to speed up the process without being used up by it. As a catalyst it can be used again and again, this year, next year, and for the generation that is still unborn. If selected and designed wisely, it won't even need many repairs or remodelings. The students with whom the tool is to be used will change and improve, for they are called to a life of transformation by the renewal of their minds.

IX

Self-Educated Persons?

Did you ever meet a self-educated man—the kind of person who, through hardship and cultural circumstances, only went through the fifth or sixth grade of school, who, in spite of those handicaps, pursued knowledge individually and tenaciously until he had become a truly learned and distinguished person who had taught himself practically everything he knew without the benefit of teachers?

I have heard friends talk about such persons, and I have met numerous people who were sixth grade dropouts. Some of those same people loved to learn, read widely, and were both intelligent and wise. But I have never met a person "who taught himself practically everything he knew." In fact, I have never met a person who taught himself anything!

Self-education is a commonly accepted notion in our secular culture, but it does not seem to make any great sense when we stop to analyze it. The idea that we can teach ourselves something which we do not yet know rests on the assumption that we do not need to know what we are teaching in order to teach it. If that were a valid assumption, then teachers would not need to be learned or educated in order to teach. A person who knew nothing about the theorems of algebra could legitimately be hired to teach a course in algebra. An illiterate could be hired to teach primary age children the skills of reading. A monotone could claim the right to be a voice teacher. All of which, of course, is obviously ridiculous and even dangerous.

We need to know before we can teach. If that is accepted, though, one has another insight into the fallacy of self-instruction. For, if a person already knows that which he is to teach, then it is totally unnecessary for him to teach himself, for he would already have learned and his efforts would merely constitute a review of prior learning.

A former professor, who taught at Michigan State University where he studiously disguised his Christian convictions, one day presented the idea of a teaching-learning continuum. He boldly asserted that teaching always implies learning and learning always implies teaching. The two processes, he claimed, are always on a continuum and can never occur independently. He intuitively sensed that he had grasp of a cardinal truth, but he was not prepared for the chorus of objections, mine included.

What about the drone who stands in front of a class day after day, purporting to teach, but hearing the student complaints that they had learned nothing? That thrust was met by a series of counter-arguments: (1) if the students had actually learned nothing, the person up front had never taught and was collecting his pay under false pretenses; (2) the students had probably learned something, but not as much or in the precise manner that they desired; (3) the students had built up so many barriers that they were now unteachable.

Next argument? What about the child who goes to a secluded corner of the library and reads books and magazines, claiming to have learned a great deal? What about the avid and discerning hermit who watches all the good TV programs, reads newspapers voraciously, and finishes two good books a week? What about the youngster who lives in a remote area of Montana, far from any school, but hikes in the woods each day and knows more about nature than most kids in Chicago or Philadelphia?

The professor was non-plussed and the class could have been tabbed a disaster. But that opening assertion would not die for lack of clear answers. It came back to haunt me every time I tried to explain the relationship between learning and teaching. The eureka experience occurred one day as I pondered the second article in the Belgic Confession of Faith, a Calvinistic document first drafted in 1562. The clue lay, clearly, in understanding the nature of God's revelation. God reveals Himself in two ways, first of all through a general revelation which encompasses all of created reality. Second, God reveals Himself in a special way through the Holy Bible. Scripture teaches plainly, and the Confession was merely repeating, that God reveals Himself through the beauty of trees and animals, through His servants, and through the splendor of a rainbow. There lay the answer, in the obvious concept of media. The trees, the birds, the mountains, the animals, and the Scriptures were simply *media through which* God imparted knowledge and insight and understanding from His omniscient storehouse. A further examination of Scripture then revealed countless other passages where God was proclaimed as the source of all knowledge and the one Great Teacher who gives to all men liberally.

In that concept of media lay the answer to the other arguments, too. The library books, the magazines, the newspapers, the TV programs, and the radio were simply types of media through which people, acting as indirect teachers, communicated with other persons, acting as learners. The person who writes script for a TV news program is then a teacher, temporarily storing his information and analysis of a current event on a tape or printed page, which material, in due time will be transmitted to a multitude of receivers, through which many people will learn. So, also, with the textbook or magazine writer and the radio or TV announcer. Looked at from the student's view, the teacher was not really missing, only hidden from observation behind the pages of the magazines and books being read.

But what about the boy in the woods? Ah, there comes the rub, where the Christian has answers and the non-Christian is stumped. Who wrote the script for the bark of the tree or the petals of the flower? Who teaches there, where the boy obviously learns? If the immanent, infinite, omniscient God of the Scriptures is rejected or replaced with some deistic machine, there are no answers of course. The Christian, though, knowing that he can do nothing without God's help, is ready to give thanks to Him for all the insight and understanding and wisdom which he has received.

Some Questions to Consider:

1. If teaching and learning are part of a continuum, would it be truthful to say that teaching is an interpersonal activity? If so, what are the ramifications of that statement?

2. If teaching is always an interpersonal activity, what must the teacher know about the learner or the recipient?

3. Some teachers feel that it is dangerous to know too much about the student? How should this argument be met?

4. What happens to role assignments when the designated learner knows more about a given subject than the designated teacher? What psychological adjustments must the novice teacher make under those conditions?

5. What dangers are there in our modern practices of reducing information about students to computerized data?

6. What advantages were there in the old one-room schoolhouses where teachers taught all the grades? What advantages does the self-contained classroom have over the compartmentalized school?

X

Conclusion

What is the nature and purpose of education? That is the basic question which educational philosophers everywhere seek to answer. It is the question to which we, too, have addressed ourselves in the foregoing pages. Not every teacher and not many parents concern themselves with such thoughts, for they are often too enmeshed in immediate activities, focusing instead on the record of the football team, the last batch of arithmetic papers to come home, or the seemingly stupid decisions the principal just made. Educational philosophy, the majority seem to believe, is for eggheads and those who have lost touch with reality.

Such should not be the case, for everyone involved with education has a philosophy or set of ideas about what the schools should be and do. Many times that philosophy is not clearly articulated; often, too, it is neither consistent or complete. In the game of philosophy, most teachers and most parents are rank amateurs, with little or no pretense toward professional status. Because these are the prevailing attitudes in our current culture, we have addressed ourselves to those questions and concerns which are most controversial and yet easiest to comprehend. We have deliberately looked, too, at some of the issues where Christians and non-Christians part company, for there are obvious differences in perspective which give continued warranty to separate Christian schools. Whereas secular educators have historically vacillated between child-centered and subject-centered schools, we have tried to demonstrate that God-centered education is more than a hollow cliche.

God-centered education offers a perspective which is big enough to bring into focus every type of instruction, whether that occur informally on the streets of the city or formally in a seminary, a law school, or the nearest school of cosmetology. Education, the Christian concludes, is not limited to that which occurs in the conventional high school, but is part and parcel of life, taking place whenever persons teach and learn. Christian education, in fact, is wholly interwoven with faith and synonymous with that edification and sanctification which God requires of His elect.

The Christian perspective, additionally, offers new and exciting slants on the questions of authority and truth, asserting, as it does, that authority and truth are gifts from God and not acquired by dint of human insight or temporal position. So, too, with relativism, a term often and erroneously claimed to be the domain of the pragmatist and existentialist. True relativism, however, can only be properly understood when every concept and every event is seen in relationship to the God who made and controls the entire universe. Here, truly, God is central, claiming that all else is relative to Him.

In the daily operation of the schools, the clearest demarcation between the Christian and the non-Christian classroom can be seen in the choice of objectives and the relative values assigned to each. The child must not only be taught to read and to write, but, more importantly, he must learn to obey, to discern between truth and falsehood, to love his neighbor, and to talk with his God in meaningful prayer. An hour's visit to the classroom of a vibrant Christian teacher will readily reveal this difference of values and objectives, even though there are many common ends, shared jointly by all.

Authentic education, according to the Christian perspective, rejects the tenets of humanism, secularism, and traditionalism, recognizing instead that God is the source and center and end of all learning, for all knowledge comes from the all-knowing God. Not all would agree, naturally, for not all men proclaim God as sovereign Lord, denying His

86

universal kingship and preferring to live as rebel bands in a world which they claim is their own. The Christian, by contrast, recognizes that he is not his own, but belongs to his faithful Savior, from whom all blessings flow.